"With honest self-disclosure, a dash quest for Truth, *Victorious Secret* is any woman trying to cope with real-world challeng... while growing ever closer to her true source of strength: an unconditionally loving God."
— Lisa M. Hendey, Founder of CatholicMom.com
and author of *The Grace of Yes*

"As a mom of three, including two boys widely spaced in age, I've survived all sorts of war games. Laura Phelps's book goes beyond plastic-sword-and-Nerf-bullet warfare and takes on the spiritual battles moms face — battles that have consequences much deeper than the pain from stepping on a Lego. Catholic women need battle plans, swords, shields, and armor; learn how to get it here."
— Barb Szyszkiewicz, O.F.S.,
editor, CatholicMom.com

"It's not easy being a woman. For that matter, it's not easy being human. Laura Mary Phelps not only embraces this, she shaves it into small pieces, froths it up into a charming drink, and offers it to each of us as an opportunity to grow closer to God. *Victorious Secret* is a gift to every woman I know: It's filled with humor and wisdom, and don't say I didn't warn you not to drink and read (lest you find yourself snorting that drink while you guffaw). Beneath the laughs, though, lies truth and humility, and it's a clarion call to each of us: The fight is worth it and the battles are not fought alone!"
— Sarah Reinhard, author and co-editor
of *The Catholic Mom's Companion to Prayer*

"Get ready to stand side-by-side with your sisters in Christ to emerge victorious on the spiritual battlefield.

"Laura Mary Phelps arms us with practical weapons for spiritual warfare seeking to silence the voices of the devil and drown out the noise that keeps us from the truth — we are 'beautiful, beloved daughters of God, an absolute masterpiece, a stunning work of art.'

"With candor and humor, Phelps takes us from the bottom of an empty tortilla chip bag into the mess of daily living, with a step-by-step format to empower women in the everyday spiritual battles we all face. With chapters on marriage, self-image, boredom, purpose, calling and trusting in God's plan for you, Phelps points us toward Mary's example and shows us the wonder of bringing ourselves to the foot of the cross, where we find 'grace upon grace ... to fight and win this battle.'"

— Cathy G. Knipper, Catholic publicist

"With her characteristic humor and insight into the heart of a woman, Laura Phelps lets us know we are not alone. But *Victorious Secret* doesn't just make you laugh out loud, it goes deep and helps make sense of the craziness in life. Loaded with practical tools and advice from someone who has been there, this book is a perfect companion on the quest to flourish and thrive as a beloved daughter of God. If you read just one book this year, may this be it!"

— Lisa Brenninkmeyer, Founder and Chief
Purpose Officer of Walking with Purpose

VICTORIOUS SECRET

Victorious SECRET

EVERYDAY BATTLES AND HOW TO WIN THEM

LAURA MARY PHELPS

Our Sunday Visitor

www.osv.com
Our Sunday Visitor Publishing Division
Our Sunday Visitor, Inc.
Huntington, Indiana 46750

Our Sunday Visitor Publishing Division
Our Sunday Visitor, Inc.
200 Noll Plaza
Huntington, IN 46750
1-800-348-2440

ISBN: 978-1-68192-264-5 (Inventory No. T1951)
eISBN: 978-1-68192-265-2
LCCN: 2018936562

Cover and interior design: Lindsey Riesen
Cover art: Shutterstock

PRINTED IN THE UNITED STATES OF AMERICA

About the Author

LAURA MARY PHELPS is first and foremost a beloved daughter of God who needed to crash and burn before realizing it. Rescued by Jesus and determined to lead women to their true identity in Christ, she works as a regional area coordinator and social media contributor at Walking with Purpose, a women's Catholic Bible study. A wife and the mother of four, she enjoys speaking to groups of women about her faith and writing at her own personal blog, www.lauramaryphelps .com, where she is free to talk about the mess she was, the mess she still is, and the God who shows up every day to clean it all up. Her minivan is filthy, and the side doors don't always open, but praise be to God for children who can climb over seats and a husband who knows how to fix things. It's not all good, but it is all grace.

This book is dedicated to the countless friends and blog readers who constantly asked, "When are you writing a book?" as well as my awesome, supportive, and loving husband, Nick, along with my beautiful children, Jack, Belle, Annie, and Luke ... who didn't mind eating "cheese bread" for dinner every night for months, because I was too busy writing to cook.

(Actually, who am I kidding? Book or no book, I would have still served them "cheese bread." Cooking is not my gift.)

And thank you, Jesus, my Savior, Healer, and Redeemer. For every bit of the mess, and the grace to use it for good.

Contents

Foreword

*"And of what should we be afraid? Our captain on this battlefield is
Christ Jesus. We have discovered what we have to do.
Christ has bound our enemies for us and weakened them that they
cannot overcome us unless we so choose to let them. So we must fight
courageously and mark ourselves with the sign of the
most Holy Cross."*
— SAINT CATHERINE OF SIENA

Following Jesus is not for the faint of heart. The day-to-day
battles that intersect the life of a daughter of God make
binge-watching Netflix very appealing. Many women settle
for superficiality and a life of comfort. Not Laura Phelps. This
warrior mama is most definitely not standing on the sidelines.
She's in the thick of the battle, each and every day.

This is why I listen to Laura's advice. Quite honestly, I
don't want to hear platitudes or principles from someone who
doesn't understand what it's like to be face down in the mud
and still choose to get back up and keep going. Laura knows
what she's talking about, and this girl has got both grit and
wisdom. Both those things come to us in spades in the pages
of *Victorious Secret*. She has lived these truths — she has applied
them first herself, and only passes on to us what works.

Here's my favorite thing: she does it all with the best
humor. No matter how dire things might get, Laura can frame

it in a way that makes you laugh. This is so important! We take ourselves so seriously ... too seriously. The ability to laugh at ourselves makes such a difference. The gift of being able to laugh with Laura is like a turbo boost of hope and energy. Personally, Laura has lightened my load by her wit and well-timed texts countless times. Now I have a collection of her thoughts, so I can return to them and both laugh and be inspired whenever I'd like. This is a treasure.

Being on the battlefield alongside Laura is a privilege. She loves sacrificially and heroically. A warrior who doesn't just defend her ground, Laura moves forward and takes back territory that the enemy thought was his. She is a force to be reckoned with, and she will not be silenced. Her strength comes from Jesus, and she stays connected to him like he's her oxygen mask. Because he is. He is her all in all. I have seen this — not just at Mass or when she's on stage talking about her faith. I've observed this when she's in the pit, when the circumstances of her life are anything but what she wants. It's in those places that she remains faithful to her Lord, convinced that the victory will always be his.

Why is she able to do this with such unbelievable perseverance, courage, and fire? I believe it's because she knows who is the captain on the battlefield. She knows that it is Jesus who commands her, but that he never does it from a distance. He is with her, in her, around her. He defends her when she is weary. He catches her when she falls. He binds her enemies, brushes the dirt off her face, and says, "You draw near this day to battle against your enemies: let not your heart faint; do not fear, or tremble, or be in dread of them; for the LORD your God is he that goes with you, to fight for you against your enemies, to give you the victory" (Dt 20:3–4).

I pray that you'll read *Victorious Secret: Everyday Battles and How to Win Them* with a pen in hand. You'll find countless practical tips that will give you the wisdom and focus to face the days that are a little tough. Your burdens will be lifted and your heart will feel lighter as Laura makes you laugh, cry, and long for a deeper relationship with Christ. But she won't just leave you with a longing; she'll direct you to simple ways you can change your yearning for God into a personal encounter with him. Get ready to enjoy the ride with Laura alongside you.

Lisa Brenninkmeyer
Founder and Chief Purpose Officer
Walking with Purpose

Chapter 1

THE EVERYDAY BATTLE

"You draw near this day to battle against your enemies:
let not your heart faint; do not fear, or tremble, or be in dread of
them; for the LORD your God is he that goes with you, to fight for
you against your enemies, to give you the victory."
— DEUTERONOMY 20:3

Have you ever felt such unrest, such anxiety building, and you had no idea where it was coming from, or how to make it go away?

This happened to me, seemingly out of the blue, one beautiful summer afternoon. Because I had already polished off the chips and salsa (and it was too early to pour myself a glass of wine), I searched for a more appropriate distraction and settled on a trip to the movie theater. I pulled up the show times for *Wonder Woman*, the anxiety still ever present, and was stopped in my tracks as the headline appeared before me:

"*Power. Grace. Wisdom. Wonder.*"

Without further hesitation, I grabbed my bag, I grabbed my son, and off we went to the 3:00 p.m. showing. My anxiety came along with me, too, and I was certain I would be charged a third ticket for it, because *that* is how big it had grown.

As I drove, I whispered that headline, almost like a prayer. *Power. Grace. Wisdom. Wonder.*

Four simple, beautiful words that quite literally moved me. Four incredible adjectives that immediately brought to mind a woman I know and love.

And yeah — no, sorry — I am *not* talking about Beyonce.

I am talking about *the* Woman of wonder, our gracious Queen and Mother, the Blessed Virgin Mary. You see, at that time, I was on day 26 of *33 Days to Morning Glory: A Do-It-Yourself Retreat in Preparation for Marian Consecration*, so Mary was heavy on my mind and heart. What is consecration, you might ask? Well, in short, consecrating oneself to Mary is simply a way to grow closer to Jesus, through his mother. Sound crazy? Yeah. Well, no argument here, because both times I have chosen to consecrate myself, my life has been hit by a raging and violent storm, and I've been thrown into some of the deepest, most troubling waters I have ever known. I know, I should stop doing this, right? But I can't. I actually look forward to it.

That's the catch when you encounter someone like Jesus — when you have truly been rescued by our Savior. *You keep on following him.* No matter how strong the winds blow against you, or how hard those waves crash fear upon you, you still get up and you follow. Still, you seek out more of him. It's sort of like a bag of really good tortilla chips. You can't eat just one. Right? You must devour the entire bag.

And I'm not some sort of martyr here, if that is what this sounds like. Chip obsessed? Yes, absolutely. But *not* a martyr. Or a masochist. Honestly. I do not follow because I love to feel like every bit of my life and very self is under some sort of hideous attack. Nor do I get up and follow because I enjoy suffering to the point of death. I certainly do not declare myself a Christ-follower because Catholics are a bunch of insane people who thrive on personal torture — which, well, is sort of true — and I want to be a part of that club. Rather,

I choose to follow daily because abiding in Jesus Christ is the only path that leads me to anywhere worth being, the only place I belong.

Trust me, I have a bookshelf of journals at home filled with the details of wrong paths taken, and they read like horror stories or depressing novels. The one thing they all have in common? They are all *me*, following *my will*. Little of God and what he might have planned for me. No turning to Jesus and asking him what I should do. Just me, on the battlefield, thinking I could figure it out all on my own.

Those journals don't end well.

Really, it's only by the grace of God that I was finally able to admit that I was in no position to write my own story, and that I needed God and his strength to guide me through this battlefield otherwise known as my life. When I decided to live a Christ-centered life, the cataracts began to clear from my self-centered eyes. I recognized that I am truly nothing — and I mean *nothing* — without him, and that apart from him, I cannot fight the everyday battle that I constantly find myself at the center of. That without him, I make some pretty stupid choices and either end up with a heart full of regret and shame, or with a precious loved one that I have injured, or (the worst-case scenario) completely out of chips and salsa. If I do not intentionally seek out relationship with my Father every single second of every single day, I may even fail to recognize that I'm in a battle or under attack. And oh, sweet friend, there is nothing more dangerous than standing on the front line, oblivious to the fight, armed with nothing.

So, back to Mary. Why does she matter? Well, think about it. She is God's Mother. As a mother myself, I would say that no person living on earth knows any of my children better than I do. For nine months our hearts beat side by side, and to this day I swear I can still feel the weight of each of my babies' hearts pressed upon mine. So what better, faster way to seek God, to know him, to grow closer to him, than by going *to and through* his mother? And maybe — and this is just a thought here — but maybe the suffering that boils up to the surface in these weeks of intentional prayer and consecration are actually necessary. Maybe God uses this time to strengthen me and to increase my trust in him. Maybe this is just the trial I need to practice the faithfulness that always precedes the blessing.

You cannot deny that suffering is a given, right? You cannot deny that battles will rage on, no matter who you are or where you live. And you cannot deny that no matter how hard we try to make this journey we are on free of any discomfort, and no matter what measures we take to remove anything remotely unpleasant or challenging, we *will* encounter suffering. So yes, we can agree that there is suffering, and we can agree that there is a battle, but how we choose to fight is up to us individually.

If I believe in God (which I do), and if I believe that my life has purpose (which it does), and if I trust that God wastes nothing (which he does not), then my suffering must have purpose, too. We cannot avoid pain in our lives, but we can choose how to steward that pain. This is why I turn to Mary. To learn from her. To learn how to respond to unspeakable pain out of love, rather than fear. To learn from her how to stand courageously at the foot of the cross, rather than curled up in the fetal position underneath the dining room table, which I may or may not have actually done … this week. To learn from her how to be a real super woman: a woman of power and grace, wisdom and wonder. The choice is ours.

So, with a large tub of popcorn — and by the way, my apologies to the concessions girl for suggesting they re-name their size descriptions, because I realize now that she probably has very little pull in the AMC marketing decision process. But honestly, what woman feels good about ordering and eating a *tub* of anything? Maybe a tub of kale. But that's not part of the $90 combo deal I ordered. I suggested they call it a *grande popcorn*. Like Starbucks. Sounds so much better, right? She thought I was crazy.

So, anyway, there I sat with my son, with our grande popcorn and sugar-free soda, next to the nest of anxiety and unexplainable fear lodged deep within my heart, praying that this movie would be just the distraction I needed, and that it would supply me with an abundance of comfort and send me home in peace. Yes. I wanted the miracle. I wanted the easy fix. I wanted to sit and be entertained and leave feeling all better.

Well, it didn't. And I didn't.

Send me home in peace, that is.

Fix me fast and easy.

But it did do something else. Something quite unexpected.

Wonder Woman awakened in me the desire to fight harder for that peace. She encouraged me to persevere. To endure. To be stronger. To be braver. To be a loud voice.

To be motivated by compassion. To show mercy. *And to do absolutely everything out of love.* (The movie also inspired me to lose weight, grow my hair out, and get lip injections, because good grief, two hours of staring at Gal Gadot on the screen is not easy for those who battle with their self-image. But that's another chapter.)

Self-loathing aside, this movie knocked hard on the door of my heart and broke me open, unleashing tears that seemed to have been building up for weeks but had nowhere to go. Of course, if you ask my children, they will roll their eyes and tell you that I cry at everything. And, well, it is true. I am totally a crier. I cry at commercials. I cry listening to music. I cried when I saw Chip and Joanna Gaines' merchandise at Target. I always cry when I have to make dinner (and so does my family). I even cried (and when I say cried, I mean sobbed uncontrollably) at the movie *Marmaduke*, which I will admit is super pathetic because Marmaduke is a fictional dog, and the plot line was quite possibly the lamest ever, and well, did *you* go to see *Marmaduke*? No? Exactly. So, yeah. I cry.

But the tears this time were valid, because they confirmed a truth I know, but had forgotten, because of that whisper that does not leave me alone. EVER. The tears were born out of the hard reality that the nest of anxiety I brought to the theater was not the problem. The fear lodged deep inside of me leaving me paralyzed was not actually the issue. The tears washed me of the lies about who I am and what I'm about and led me away from the anxiety and the fear and back to its very source, back to the rulers of the present darkness and the one behind the evil schemes, back to the one I was facing in battle: the devil.

Yes. I said it. The devil. And in the very first chapter, too. I'm bold like that. Because we hate to talk about him, don't we? Well, let's get over that. Because this book is about battles, and a battle always has an enemy, and ours is the devil. Do not be fooled into thinking the enemy is your annoying coworker, or your opinionated mother-in-law, or those extra fifteen pounds you can't seem to lose, or your difficult child, or your disappointing bank account, or that perfect friend's always perfect status on Facebook, or your disengaged spouse. "For we are not contending against flesh and blood, but against the principalities, against the powers, against the world rulers of this present darkness, against the spiritual hosts of wickedness in the heavenly places" (Eph 6:12). Evil is real and so is the devil, and he, the father of lies, is the one Jesus said comes to "steal and kill and destroy" (Jn 10:10). He is the enemy that we are up against. And the sooner we accept that, the better prepared we are to fight, and not just fight — but win. Because that's the goal here, right? To be victorious.

I think we all know we are in an everyday battle. I am not revealing some earth-shattering, breaking news. But I am not convinced we fully comprehend how powerful this battle is, and the ruin it can leave us in. And I am certain that too many of us are marching into war completely unprepared because we tend to be so self-focused that we fail to remember *everyone else* is in a battle, too. Everyone we love, everyone we know, everyone we disagree with on Twitter, everyone we will never meet this side of heaven. And I can't help but wonder if maybe we would throw fewer stones, and instead dole out more grace, if we could remember this truth.

Perhaps if we prayed for each other instead of rolling our eyes, or slamming on our horn, or quickly reacting and hitting *send*, or making an unkind comment under our breath because the woman at the cash register takes forty minutes to scan one freaking bag of instant rice, and you have fifty-six more items to scan and need to be somewhere in ten minutes. Perhaps we would be that people of peace we claim we want to be if we remembered everyone else was in a battle. We would certainly be a more compassionate and patient people if we were to see our brothers and sisters this way: as warriors on the same team, in the same fight, just trying to stay alive. Sure, scanning a bag of instant rice should not take longer than it does to cook it. But even the rice-scanning-challenged are facing a battle, and not just alone, but with us. With me. With you. With that annoying person on Twitter. Don't you see? We are called to stand side by side. Shoulder to shoulder. Shield to shield. We are more powerful when we do this. We stand a better chance of … well … *standing* if we stand together. The arrows do not discriminate; they fly at all of us. Do you really believe you are strong enough to withstand them?

I believe that you are. I believe that all women have wonder woman strength and beauty and courage and wisdom within. We may not carry a physical shield and sword (and thank God for that, because my shoulder already hurts from the giant Jessica Simpson purse I carry around). But we *can* put on the armor of God. Every single day, when we wake up, before we reach for our phone, or take out the dog, or pour that first cup of coffee, or sit at our computer, even go to the bathroom, we *should* put on the armor of God.

> Therefore, take the whole armor of God, that you may be able to withstand in the evil day, and having done all, to stand. Stand therefore, having fastened the belt of truth around your waist, and having put on the breastplate of righteousness, and having shod your feet with the equipment of the gospel of peace; besides all these, taking the shield of faith, with which you can quench all the flaming darts of the Evil One. And take the helmet of salvation, and the sword of the Spirit, which is the word of God. (Eph 6: 13–17)

The enemy would love for us to quit fighting and to stay stuck in our circumstances. That is where he had me that beautiful summer day. Stuck. Locked in my anxiety. Focused on my fear. Believing the lie that I was in this alone and too weak to prevail. And maybe that is you, too. Or was you. Or will be you. Maybe your desire to persevere is so buried beneath the lies you somehow, sometime started to believe, that the very thought of standing up and dressing for battle feels like a battle in its own right. But I am here to say that you can stand. No matter how weary, no matter how burdened, no matter how afraid, no matter how big and impossible that mountain before you appears. You can do this.

How do I know? Well, because I, sweet friend, have failed at so much. I have reached for the wrong weapons this world has handed me, and I have allowed the flaming arrows to pierce me more times than I care to admit. And because I was too distracted by the whisper of this world and its empty promises, I failed to hear the voice of truth, and I followed the lie alone into battle way too many times.

And it did not go well.

But that's okay. Because my journey, your journey … it is far from over. And God's grace and mercy? They are fresh and new each and every morning. We can do this. We really can. Trust me. Actually, that is an awful idea. Don't trust me. But let's work on trusting him. Because he is our weapon. His word. His truth. He is our peace. He is our Savior and our Defender, and the One in control. So winning really isn't so much about *our* defeating the enemy as it is about surrendering to God who has already defeated and won. It's about standing with Mary at the foot of the cross, freeing our hands by dropping our mess at his feet, and choosing to pick up the armor of Christ instead, trusting that he will set it all right, believing that he will lead us safely through the battle, drawing our strength from him alone.

What do you say you get up and get dressed, and meet me on the front line?

Ladies, we have a battle to win.

BATTLE PLAN

Maybe the battle you are in is crystal-clear. Or maybe this is the first time you ever considered there *is* a battle. Maybe you are confused because you thought this book was about coffee and lingerie. Whatever the case, stick with me, and before suiting up, how about we simply spend a little quiet time with the Lord asking him, "What attack am I unaware of? What battle am I losing? How can I fight stronger?"

WEAPON OF CHOICE

Throughout this book, I will suggest weapons appropriate for the fight. As we have just begun to march forward together, let's take today to get out our Bible (or buy a Bible, or wipe the dust off the Bible, or finally throw out that dried carnation wrist corsage from your 1988 prom that has been pressed between wax paper in your Bible) and open to the book of Ephesians, chapter 6, verses 10–17. Pray with God's Word, making note of your new wardrobe, which we will be drawing from in each chapter of this book. (Don't worry, it comes with shoes.)

Chapter 2

THE SELF-IMAGE BATTLE

*"Let not yours be the outward adorning with braiding of hair,
decoration of gold, and wearing of robes, but let it be the hidden
person of the heart with the imperishable jewel of a gentle and quiet
spirit, which in God's sight is very precious."*
— 1 PETER 3:3–4

I was feeling pretty good about life and my place in it, until I scrolled through my Instagram feed and saw it.

The pie.

This perfectly baked cherry pie.

And not only was it a beautiful and delicious-looking pie, but taken out of it was the perfect little bite. This glorious, gourmet cherry pie was plated on a perfectly worn piece of vintage china, with a single silver fork, gracefully placed on the edge of the plate. And as if that were not enough, this entire plate and pie was photographed on a rustic, distressed, and absolutely fabulous farm table.

Now, some people might scroll right past that pie. Because I mean, honestly, who cares? Big deal. You made yourself a pie and took a picture of it. Congratulations. Whatever. But not me. You want to know the bag of crazy that popped into my mind when I saw that beautiful pie?

How on earth did she have the time to bake that? Why did she bake it? Obviously, she must be having a party or a group of friends over. Or one of her fabulous arts and crafts gatherings. I'll bet she is sitting in her perfect house right now laughing with friends and being all hospitable, and her hair probably looks good, too. Good grief, she has people over in the middle of the day? How is her house clean enough for that? And that china plate ... she probably got it at a thrift shop. And where does all of her money come from anyway? She has nineteen kids, and she doesn't even work! I guess she sits around baking and entertaining and thrifting ... while I sit in my mess of a rented home, microwaving some sort of loser dinner for my family on paper plates because all of our real plates are chipped and sitting in the sink. And what about all those kids? They probably helped bake the darn thing! In fact, I'll bet they picked the cherries that went into that pie as a family because this was some sort of homeschooling lesson, where they measured and counted and turned pie baking into an educational experience. They probably held hands and prayed over the ingredients. And why don't I have a farm table? I think I need a farm table. Seriously. I think I would be so much happier if I just found the right farm table. I hate myself. I really do. I mean look at me. I'm wearing my 13-year-old's leggings and my 11-year-old's dirty sweatshirt. I look like a homeless woman. I really do. If I sat outside on the corner you would totally give me money. That's how homeless I look right now. And what really gets me is, what woman can sit down and eat a pie on a Tuesday afternoon without hating herself? Right? I mean come on, it's gotta be loaded with gluten. And sugar. So much sugar. But she's so skinny! So unfair. She's skinny eating pie with friends in her clean home while I sit at my messy desk in my homeless attire. You know how fat I would get if I did nothing but make pies and eat them? She probably doesn't even eat it.

She's probably one of those women who invite other women to come over and eat, and she sits and watches. She wants everyone to be fatter than she is. Nice. Ugh. I really am a mess. Why can't I just get myself together? The house is a mess, my desk is a mess, I am not even good at my job, and who knows what my kids are up to? I need help. Serious help. And I need a farm table. I really need a farm table. What's wrong with me? I hate that stupid pie.

Ah, the wonderful, encouraging world of social media! Isn't it great?

Only, the problem here really isn't social media, is it? The problem here is me. How I view and compare myself to others. How I distort images and do some serious magical thinking, which is a therapist term for "making up a story and fully believing it." Because other than the fact that this woman had a few minutes and the desire to photograph a pie, every other thought that ran through my head was most likely false. *(Except for the thrifting. I stand by the thrifting, because honestly, I may not know her, but she thrifts too much.)*

But we do this, don't we? We see an image and our minds create a story around it. We *see*, and we *desire*. And this is good. A great picture ought to tell a story; it ought to stir emotion. But there is a problem with this today. Because we are bombarded by images, and we have the hideous ability to see what everyone is doing, eating, drinking, wearing, vacationing, and enjoying, at *every given moment of our every single day*. And most of the images we see? Guess what? *They are filtered. They are staged. They are untrue.* They are the one perfect shot out of 500 others you did not see, and most likely never will.

But it is hard to choose not to use filters, because they really do make us look so much better. The first time I used a filter on my face and saw the even, smooth skin and bright eyes, I was sold! And don't even get me started on those animal filters my children use ... because honestly, I am at my most beautiful ever when I look and sound like a deer. Who knew?

Strange, but I gotta admit, so true. So much so, that I have already requested that when I die, if possible, I'd like to be laid out in the coffin looking exactly like that deer.

Let's just confess. We all love filters. And let's just admit that if we like ourselves better as seen through an animal filter, well, sweet friend, there might be a problem.

Because here is an interesting thing. You know what it means to filter? I do. Not because I am smart, but because I looked it up. To use a filter means to "*remove what is unwanted.*" When I read that, I was really struck by it, and not in a good way. Something about the word *remove* ... something about the word *unwanted.* How many years of my life have I devoted to trying to remove those things about me that I do not want, those things about me that I think make me less attractive? Less desirable? Those things in my life that might point to the fact that I am kind of a hot mess and not the perfect woman I'd like you to think that I am? *Too many years.* From the nose job when I was just seventeen, to drastic weight loss in college, to the frantic house-cleaning maniac I turn into moments before company arrives. I have been on a nearly life-long quest of seeking out the illusion of perfection. Changing my image to fit whatever crowd I was currently in, transforming myself into the woman I thought a man would be attracted to. And let's be honest, ladies, we not only like to be perfect for the men, but even more so for other women. Right? We are the most competitive species I know, and we love a good game of comparison — as long as we win. So, all of this filtering we do, it really isn't about enhancing the beauty that is already there, is it? No. It is about removing the unwanted to give the illusion that everything is so much better than it actually is, because the way we are, as is, is not good enough.

I think we do this because we want everyone to believe that we are better than just okay. I think we remove and sift and filter things out so that people cannot see what is really going on inside our homes, inside our families, inside our marriages, inside our hearts, inside our heads. I get it, not everyone needs to see the inside of your kitchen junk drawer, or what your linen closet looks like. And not everyone should be trusted with the truth of how weary you feel, how painfully lonely your marriage has been, how lost you fear your children might be, how you struggle to find meaning and purpose. But we do need to recognize that filters don't work in real life and in real relationships, because filters don't encourage the basic things we need to thrive, like truth, authenticity, and honesty.

And we really need to acknowledge, at some point, that life is not perfect, we are not perfect, and that our pain is valid and real and okay and should be addressed, because sticking a deer's ears and nose on it will not make it go away. It's a temporary fix. It is not made to last. And I don't know about you, but no matter how loud the world gets, or how much it tries to convince me that nothing lasts forever, and love is a feeling, and we can choose our gender and marry our dog (okay, so we can't marry our dog ... yet), I still disagree. I disagree because I want authentic, lasting relationships, and I want to choose to love because I desire the greatest good for others, not just myself, and because I want to live in the light of truth. But if I can't be honest with myself, how will I ever learn to be honest with others? And if I can't truly love myself, how can I truly love others? All these filters, all this work to appear lovely, all the botox and tummy tucks and nose jobs, only tear us away and apart from our true selves, from the truth of not only who we are, but *whose* we are: each of us is a beautiful, beloved daughter of God, an absolute masterpiece, a stunning work of art.

That is exactly how you describe yourself, isn't it? God's beloved. A work of art. (Did you laugh when you read that, or roll your eyes? Because I did both while I wrote it.)

It's hard to believe this, isn't it? It's hard to get real. I think we have just pretended for so long that it feels wrong to drop our mask and widen the camera lens and show the whole picture. But here is the thing. There will never be a filter we can use that will keep our true selves from the One who sees all, knows all, and created all. And I often wonder what God thinks when he sees us poring over false images, doubting who we are, buying into lies, comparing our lives to one another, trying to remake ourselves to look like someone else. I think about how sad he must feel when we pick apart our faces, our bodies, our marriages, our families, our careers, our lives, desperately trying to cover up the imperfections, remove the unwanted. And oh, how exhausted we are. How painfully tired we are from all of this performing. From all of this nonsense. From all of these empty attempts at identifying ourselves as anything other than "child of God." Because the bottom line is just that. We are his beloved. We are his creation. He made us to love him and to know him here on earth, so that we can live for an eternity with him in heaven. It really is so simple.

And yet, we have made it so incredibly complicated. The world has shoved an endless buffet of self-image choices in our face, telling us we can pick who we are, remake ourselves completely, choose our identity and what we want to be. And I will be honest. I have been up and down that buffet for forty-seven years now. Turns out, finding suggestions on how to change myself, to better myself, to improve who I am apart from a relationship with God is super easy! But finding the truth about my identity? Finding the one thing that tells me to stop striving, to stop self-loathing, to rest in the arms of my Father because I have been made in his image, and because he loves me, just as I am? Not so easy. The choice that reminds me that my self-worth is not wrapped up in my appearance, successes, how big or clean my house is, or by the number of college acceptances and scholarships my children earn, or by that stupid, freaking number on the scale? I can't easily find that choice. And how sad. How incredibly sad that we are all running around like headless chickens, desperate for purpose, dying for meaning, running in circles of despair, because by the world's standards, our worth is nothing.

Sweet friend, this could not be any farther from the truth of who we are and the enormous value we possess. Because you see, my self-worth, and your self-worth? If we truly want to break out the measuring stick, if we honestly require an accurate weight of our worth, all we need to do is stop grasping at the empty promises around us and look up at the crucifix. Close your eyes right now for one minute and see it. See him. Because the fact is that God sent his only beloved Son to earth, to feel all that we feel, to live among us, to give up his life for sinners like you and me while he was sinless, and to die a most hideous death just for you and for me — just as we are. And he would do it all over again, even if we were the only two people on earth to die for. Do we really need more proof of how precious we are, how beautiful we are, how worth it we are, than that?

We were worth dying for. And we still are.

It is when I do this, when I take my self-doubt, my self-hatred, my hideous lack of self-worth, and the false idea that I can find my identity in anything other than Christ, to the foot of the cross, then I can see our Father reaching out to all of us, as a loving father does. And I can hear his voice saying,

> *"Oh, sweet daughter, just stop. Please stop and listen. I made you. Do you hear me? You are my beautiful creation. And you have been made perfect in my image. Not the images you see on Instagram. MY image. There is no bit of you that is unwanted. I knit you myself, and I do not make mistakes. Stop undoing the threads. It is killing you. You are exhausted. I did not make you to feel this way. Stop the striving, take off the filter, and just be you. Only I can purify you, only I can refine you. Let me. Let my light pass through you. Quit shutting me out. Put down the filter of this world and take up MY filter. Look at yourself through my eyes, and through my heart. See yourself the way I see you. See how I love you, how very much I want you. Just as you are. Every piece of you. Wanted."*

And then I hear him say, *"By the way, she bought that pie from the store and the rest of her house was a mess, and you don't need a farm table, and you want to see homeless? Because I can show you homeless … so please … just shut up."* Only God probably doesn't say shut up. I do. I should probably filter that.

I don't know. I just think we live a half-filled life when we spend it trying to make it look like something it isn't; when we spend it trying to fill it with things that do not come from God. Because honestly? Who are we fooling? God sees you, and he wants you. Every bit of the you he created. He doesn't want you looking like a deer and he doesn't care how perfect your life looks on your Instagram feed. Only he holds your purpose, and only he knows your plan. And the sooner we get to know him, who knew us before we were born, the sooner those plans will be revealed. God sees so much more than you are willing to show, and he knows the amazing things about you that he has given to only you. And he wants it all.

You are wanted as is. Made in his image. Unfiltered. Unstaged. Totally and 100 percent wanted. Look at *that* image. Post that. And believe it.

BATTLE PLAN

Let's check our "feed": those things we look at, allowing them to influence us and shape our hearts. Maybe it's social media, gossip magazines, or a favorite Netflix binge. Do a heart check and ask yourself, "Am I encouraged by what I see? Or do I want to throw myself off a cliff when I'm done?" So many of us are choosing to look at things that chip away at our self-image, dragging us down into the pit of comparison. Pay attention to how you feel after you spend time looking at these images. Maybe it is time to clean up your feed not only by eliminating the junk, but by adding more truth and beauty.

WEAPON OF CHOICE

The Belt of Truth is the first piece of armor we need to put on. This is no ordinary leather belt. You won't find it at TJ Maxx. From it will hang our Sword of the Spirit, so it is a most important piece of defense, not only protecting us against the lies that bombard us, but also preparing us for victory in the battle. I have always wanted to say this: "Gird your loins!" And while girding, go ahead and repeat often, "You are all fair, my love; there is no flaw in you" (Song 4:7), believing that these are God's words spoken to you, just as you are.

Chapter 3

THE "WHAT'S IN
IT FOR ME?" BATTLE

*"Give, and it will be given to you; good measure, pressed down,
shaken together, running over, will be put into your lap. For with the
measure you give will be the measure you get back."*
— LUKE 6:38

My favorite Gospel story is the one where the angel
Gabriel comes down to the young, sweet Virgin Mary
and announces God's plan for her, the "news of great joy": that
she will be overshadowed by the Holy Spirit, become pregnant
and give birth to the Son of God, and she will call him Jesus,
meaning, "God saves." And without hesitation, Mary looks
up to the angel, eyes wide, leans in close, and quietly asks,
"What's in it for me?"

Oh, wait.

That's not how it goes.

Actually, she said yes.

Now, if I were Mary? Well, we'd most likely have a
different story. That, I realize, would change quite a bit when
it comes to the small things, like our salvation. So, ya know,

good for you, God, for being wise enough not to send your messenger to me. Plus, if an actual angel ever did appear to me, I would be so terrified that I would, without question, die of a heart attack before the angel ever had a chance to share God's plan. I don't even answer the door when it is the UPS guy knocking. Unexpected visitors horrify me.

But let's say I didn't die on the spot. Then, yes. Before agreeing to anything, and before making some sort of sarcastic remark of this being "news of great joy," I would totally ask, *"What's in it for me?"* Because I would want to know. I mean, wouldn't you? If you were asked to give up your plans, your marriage as you had dreamed it to be, your very body, your hopes, your will, your control, and every single bit of life as you know it and desired it to be, wouldn't you sort of be curious about the payoff? Wouldn't you want to be sure that this incredible inconvenience, this unusual sacrifice, this unheard-of teen pregnancy bound to be the hot topic at the well, was going to be worth it?

Because, let's be honest here. We demand to know what the payoff is with lesser things than being asked to be *the Mother of God.* We don't usually like to put ourselves out there, or change our plans, or make ourselves vulnerable, or go the extra mile, or simply do something we don't want to do, or fully understand, unless we get some sort of reward in return. Some kind of consolation prize. I mean, our children can't poop in the potty without getting a sticker on a chart, and are we really any different? How often do we do what we do, not because we were asked, not because it is the right thing to do, not because we love the person asking, not out of obedience, not because pooping anywhere *but* the potty is actually kind of gross, but because of the hope that there is something in it for us, personally? Being told, "Well done, faithful servant" just isn't enough for us, is it? We want a sticker on our chart.

And we don't just do this with the lesser things. We do this with the big things, too. We do this with our relationships. With our spouses. Our children. Our friends. Our church. Our places of work. With our God. We haggle and we gamble and we place our bids. We try to negotiate the price down, we scheme and we finagle. We cut corners and we go down roads we were certain we would never go down, just to be sure we don't get the short end of the stick. We do everything we possibly can to get the best deal for ourselves, sometimes regardless of who gets hurt or overlooked or slighted in the process. Because unlike Mary, whose one motive was her love for God, our motive is mostly love for ourselves. And "thy will" becomes my will. And this is a dangerous place to be.

My husband and I went through a difficult season years ago (not to be confused with the difficult season we are in now, or were in many, many years ago, or will most likely be in, in another few years. If you are not yet married, my apologies for breaking the news to you, that you might not hear while testing wedding cake flavors or planning your exotic honeymoon, that marriage is one beautiful trial after beautiful trial. But please, do not be afraid. Cake and vacation do not strengthen a marriage. Trials do.).

I remember, very clearly, being at a party in conversation with a friend's husband, who decided that I was going to be the lucky person he would share all of his life's dissatisfaction with. And after running down the laundry list of what his day-to-day routine lacked, he moved on to the sacred: his wife. Maybe it was the drinks. In fact, I am sure it was the drinks. But suddenly, he was very much at ease sharing the most personal details of his marriage with me: running down the things his wife did not bring to the marital table — the lack of respect she had for him, the lack of intimacy between them, really, just the plain ol' lack. And after his rant, I remember him shaking his head and sort of smiling this sad smile of despair, if there is such a thing. Then he spoke those five deadly words out loud: *"What's in it for me?"*

Those words were not only deadly for him, but deadly for me, too. Because once floated out there, like a neon sign hanging over our heads, I started to ask that question for myself. For my own relationship. My own marriage. My own life. My own day-to-day routine. There was this shift in my heart, ever so slight, but that is all it takes, you know, to steer you off track. One small shift of the heart is something our enemy patiently waits for. And in an instant, without being aware of it, I went from thinking about how *we* could make things better for *us*, to how *I* deserved to make things better for *me*. Because when the tempter has you asking, *"What's in it for me?"* you immediately, and unknowingly, erase authentic relationship. With your spouse, with your loved ones, and most importantly, with God.

Now, just a side note here, but speaking poorly about your spouse or a loved one to another person, or sharing intimate details and feelings that truly should go no further than the ears and the heart of the one you made vows to, most especially to the opposite sex, is never a good idea. For obvious reasons. Because this is a fiery poison that will burn down necessary hedges of protection we must plant and place around our most precious relationships. Remember, the enemy hates your marriage and he hates your family, and he will do whatever it takes to destroy them. And he starts with one small shift of the heart. Sister, guard yours. With all that you have, please, guard your heart, because small fractures never remain small fractures. Eventually, they break big. So plant those hedges. And maybe stop talking after two drinks. Or maybe just one.

But Mary. Mary never asked, *"What's in it for me?"* Rather, she pondered it all in her heart. *She pondered.* How often do we ponder? Especially in response to a difficult command or calling from God that we do not understand. Honestly? I think the last time I pondered was in aisle 6, when I had to choose between the tortilla chips with a hint of jalapeño, or the tortilla chips with a hint of lime. Seriously. I spend more time pondering the useless, the stuff that in the end makes no difference whatsoever in my life here on earth, or eternally. But I give immediate, knee-jerk reactions to God when he offers me a game-changing plan, a gift disguised in discomfort, an opportunity for my heart to grow — the things that hold eternal value.

This is why we have to love and learn from Mary. She did

not doubt God's unusual plan for her. She did not look at this truly bizarre calling as a mystery that she had to solve. Rather, she agreed to it, asking to be shown how God wanted her to make it happen. And her response to this angel, this yes to her God, and everything that follows, is something so powerful, so exceptional, that I can barely wrap my selfish human mind around it. Because even at my most faithful, the fire in my heart for Jesus is more like a pathetic, flickering birthday candle than the blazing, all-consuming fire that fills Mary's heart. When God appears and calls me to do hard things, I usually blow that candle out and run for the hills. And by the hills, I mean the chips and salsa. But not Mary. Her obedience and trust fanned the fire within her, and she stayed still, pondering.

And you might wonder, did I buy the tortilla chips with the hint of jalapeño or the hint of lime? Just kidding. You don't care. But for the record, I bought and ate both.

But seriously.

You might wonder, because I sure have and often still do … *how?* How on earth does one get to this place of total trust? Of real, hard-core surrender? Of putting yourself last and others before yourself? Because every single time I think I have reached that place, every single time I say to myself, *this must be what it means to lay it all down at his feet,* every time it appears I have given all that I have to give over to my Savior, and that green pasture is just around the corner, I am slammed with another trial. I am blindsided by another blow. I am thrown into a brand new battle. I am asked to sacrifice just a little bit more. Trust a little bit more. Have a little more faith. And it is here that I throw myself on the floor, or throw something across the room, or throw that tantrum, just freaking *throw* … and I scream and I demand to know the answers to those WHY questions that, deep down inside, I know better than to ask. I will be honest: I'm one of those Catholics who prays that Rosary and lights those candles and hits those novenas and rises up early for prayer, and I still scream out to God, in anger and in sorrow, but really, mostly in anger, because honestly, don't I deserve better? Have I not proven my love? And like a projectile vomit, the ugliness violently spews out:

> *"Good grief, is this even worth it? What is your good plan, Lord, anyway? Where is your news of great joy? Because I don't see it. When does this suffering end? When will you reveal to me that great big weight of joy that you promised? Because this hardly seems good and this hardly feels worth it and news flash, Lord, but I'm not feeling the joy! Will I ever see your goodness in the land of the living? Or will I die, like Moses, old and bearded and exhausted, because I have a beard, Lord! Look! I am a grown woman with a beard! What's the deal with that? Am I just supposed to work hard and suffer and then die, so that everyone but me can enjoy all that milk and honey? Tell me now! I demand to know ... do I just need to be dead and bearded to understand any of this? To understand you? And please, Lord, tell me ... with this giant cross you have lovingly super-glued to my weak and frail back, that you claim is a gift, I would really like to know, what is the payoff? Where is my sticker? And for the love, sweet Jesus, please tell me, because I am dying to know: WHAT'S IN IT FOR ME?"*

Welcome to my inner thoughts that, really, no one ought to hear, except for Father in the confessional. Please pray for the priest who hears my confessions. Poor guy.

But I share this with you because if there is one thing that I have learned in the few years I have worked in women's ministry, it is that I am not alone. Believe it or not, I am not the only Catholic woman who takes frequent trips to crazyland aboard the selfish express. I am not the only devout woman who loves Jesus, but sometimes doesn't. Who agrees to pick up her cross daily, but wishes truly that the call was to pick it up biweekly. Or maybe even just once a month. Ideally, not at all. And I know that I am not the only faithful woman who gets so completely overwhelmed, so buried beneath it all, so distracted by the enemy and tossed by the waves, that my "yes" to God, that I desire to give, shifts ever so slightly, transforming itself into a bitter *Why?* A demanding *What?* A desperate need to understand the plan and to be assured that in the end, I will be okay.

Because I think *"What's in it for me?"* is not simply birthed out of self-centeredness, but rather out of fear. I think we are afraid to answer God's call. I think we are afraid of what he might ask us to do. I think we are afraid that if we follow Christ, we will not only have to give up those sins that we know are bad for us but think we need to get by, but we will also be asked to constantly give to others. And the fear here is that if we do that, there will be nothing left for ourselves. And I think we think this way because we forget who God is. I think we think this way because maybe we have never truly encountered him. Or we've forgotten what that encounter was really like.

You see, Mary, who was so clearly set apart from the rest of us, she knew who God was. She studied the scriptures and soaked up the Old Testament. She had come to know God in such a beautiful, intimate, and personal way. So, when asked to drop everything, when asked to trust, when called to step up to the task she was created for and born to do, nothing other than "yes" made sense. Make no mistake, yes does not mean we understand. But it does mean we have faith, regardless. Maybe if we spent more time in Scripture, getting to know our good Father, this generous and kind King, even though we may not understand the circumstances we are in, we would be less tempted to run from them. To seek out a better plan. To find an easier path. To travel a road less dangerous. To live comfortably. Because our God? He may call us to unsafe places, and he make ask us to step out of our comfort zone, but he is also a God of abundance, and he always will be. He multiplies all that we bring him, no matter how small our offering. Remember, he feeds thousands on just two fish and five loaves of bread — and even then he sends us off with leftovers. You see, when we hand over all that we have, God not only feeds us until we are satisfied, he leaves us with more to eat, he leaves us with more to share. I promise you that. He desires to give us a full life, overflowing with joy. He does not ask anything of us, unless it is for our absolute good. Yes, that is hard for us to process sometimes. I admit, I struggle greatly with this. So many battles I find myself thrown into feel so endless, so pointless, so unloving, so not for my good, that I am tempted to pull back, to close off, and to seek out another way. My own way.

There is only one true way, however, and that way is Jesus. We need to know him if we are going to work with him. We need to trust him when the messenger appears, and we need to be able to say yes to the task that God has created specifically and uniquely for us. We need to believe that our Father loves us so much that, no matter what he asks, we will not be left out of receiving the trophy that awaits us. We will not lose the battle, or walk away defeated, or not be able to walk at all. If we abide in him, we will be victorious.

Look on the bright side. Mary was already asked to give birth to Jesus, so no chance of that happening to you. But we are asked, each day, to birth Christ within us in our own way. And maybe one way we can do that is by putting *"what's in it for me?"* aside, and asking, "WHO is in it for me?" Because God is in it for you. God is in it for me. And if you are in a situation right now where you feel like maybe he has forgotten about you, please understand this: that thought does not come from God. That thought comes from the devil. Resist him. Fight him with truth. Read God's Word and know that he is in this battle with you, fighting with and for you. Kick that conductor of the selfish express on its way to crazyland to the curb and let him know that you are a beloved child of God — and you will only ride with him.

It is important that we do this. It is important that we watch our words and carefully choose who we share them with. Today, let's banish the *"What's in it for me"* attitude from our lives. Because when our "me" becomes "we" and our "I" becomes "you," beautiful, unexpected things happen. Hearts break open and are softened, relationships are strengthened, love increases, and God grows so big within us that there will barely be enough room to store all of his blessings. He gives in abundance when we respond out of love. He will supply you with all the grace upon grace you need to fight and win this battle. You will wake up to find that a "yes" to God never leaves you empty or forgotten, but rather filled to the brim and overflowing, your heart bursting with joy, with a chart full of more stickers than you ever imagined.

What's in it for you? Oh, sweet friend. So much more than you know.

BATTLE PLAN

Do you ever wonder, "What's in it for me?" Maybe you are in a relationship that feels one-sided or a job that never seems to pay off. Take some time to ponder your situation and check your motive in all things. Do you do what you do out of love of God, or do you do what you do for the prize at the bottom of the cereal box?

WEAPON OF CHOICE

It's time to break out the Sword of the Spirit. If we want to walk away from this battle victorious, marinating ourselves in the Scriptures is essential. Using this sword will take practice. Hebrews 4:12 tells us, "For the word of God is living and active, sharper than any two-edged sword, piercing to the division of soul and a spirit, of joints and marrow, and discerning the thoughts and intentions of the heart." This sword is better than a serrated bread knife, able to cut away at all of the obstacles that keep beauty and truth from our hearts.

Chapter 4

THE MARRIAGE BATTLE

"Let love be genuine; hate what is evil, hold fast
to what is good; love one another with brotherly affection;
outdo one another in showing honor."
— ROMANS 12:9

M y husband, looking completely defeated and stressed out, sadly confessed, "I didn't get you an anniversary present. I'm sorry."

I was unloading the dishwasher in my attractive, baggy sweats, wearing the slippers he had gotten me a year ago, that I had actually just duct taped back together because they were falling apart. Despite the soles that were coming off in pieces, and the well-worn holes in the knitted toes, I was doing my best to save them. Because despite the clear beating they have taken, I cling to the past, recalling the cold mornings I slipped them on and felt comforted by their warmth and protection. I cannot stand walking on hard, cold ground.

"That's okay, honey," I reassured him. "I don't even have a card for you."

You know, not too many years ago, this scenario would have really upset me. Seriously, I would have spiraled fast, and although I might have shrugged it off as "no biggie" and said, "That's okay," I would then have proceeded to throw the plates into the dishwasher hard, and slam the bathroom door behind me, just to prove, you know, how okay I really was. I mean, come on. No anniversary gift? Not even a card? These would have been taken as sure signs that our marriage was loveless, and over, and that it was probably because of that bad impulse decision to cut my long hair short because it looked so cute on Reese Witherspoon, and who doesn't love Reese Witherspoon? And when women on social media are posting their anniversary vacations? Their anniversary diamonds? Their anniversary dates and chocolates and flowers? What am I supposed to post today? My stupid, broken slippers, wrapped in duct tape?

Maybe I should.

Because today, on the anniversary of twenty-one years of marriage, the lack of material gifts and the falling apart slippers couldn't feel any more right. The total detachment from *things* given to represent how we feel, *things* received so that we can prove our love, *things* worthy of posting for the world to see, is as warm a welcome as these sad little slippers used to be. The truth is, my husband and I are in the process of real life, and doing some heavy cross lifting with and for each other. And nothing else matters. Not the date. Not the gift. Not the card. Only us, together, carrying this cross. The gift we have to give today is not dressed up in a tiny blue box with a pretty white ribbon. Instead, it's our very hearts, raw and broken open, but being held together ever so gently by grace — the grace we have learned to give each other. The grace that twenty-one years of marriage has shown us. The grace upon grace that we have been freely given through Jesus Christ. With this heaviness, with this burden, comes this deep sense of finally understanding what authentic love is. What authentic love requires. What authentic love does. What marriage is really all about. With broken slippers and broken hearts, there is still this unspeakable joy, this "grounded in truth" knowing that this marriage, messy and flawed, is undeniably blessed.

I remember sitting at my computer about nine years ago or so, back when we were younger and struggling in just about every aspect of our lives, living in beautiful, sunny Los Angeles, feeling less than sunny. Feeling less than beautiful. I was so disappointed, so unfulfilled, and I clearly recall thinking, *'Til death do us part? Good grief … death? That could be a really long time! What was I thinking when I said that?"* I'll tell you what I was thinking. I was thinking about my beautiful white dress. And the spectacular Tavern on the Green reception. And the hand-tied autumn flowers in dusty peach and linen roses. And the tragically hip black-and-white photographs. And the horse and carriage ride through NYC. And the tiramisu cake. Because when you say "'til death do us part," are you really thinking, providing you are blessed to have a long life together, what that long life will actually look like? And when you say "in sickness and in health," are you truly thinking in that moment what sickness might demand of you? And that maybe that sickness has nothing to do with you or your spouse, but possibly your child, or a parent who demands your time and care? And when you say "for richer or poorer," are you really thinking that you love this person so much that you are willing to sell your clothes and jewelry one day, just to pay rent, without feeling any resentment? Without growing bitter? And maybe you were. Maybe you will. Maybe you are. But to keep things real here, I will raise my hand high and say, that I was not. Me? I planned a fabulous wedding. I did not plan a fabulous marriage.

I am a big fan of dreaming, and one of my favorite things to do with my husband is to simply sit and dream; to think about what we could do one day, where we could go, how we could decorate a home, what might become of our children, what possibilities and plans are waiting ahead of us. And I think this is fun, and I think this is good to do. It gives us a little glimpse into our creative hearts and minds, and it can be an exciting little peek into what might one day be. But you have to be careful. There is that thrill of letting your imagination go wild and dreaming for the fun of it, and then there are unrealistic expectations we hold as truth, and the crushing disappointment that always follows when such expectations go unmet. I absolutely went into marriage with unrealistic expectations. I'm telling ya, if I could do it all over again, I would not register for that stupid bread maker. Instead, I would register for realistic expectations. Not sure what department you find that in. Maybe somewhere between the fine china and toilet bowl scrub brush.

But that's the thing! How many of us register for anything remotely practical? Bread maker? Suddenly now that I am a wife, buying a loaf of bread isn't acceptable? I need to be making my bread? Waffle makers that are heart-shaped? Seven hundred place settings of fine china that I will never use because it is too good to use? Pots and pans that cost more than a car? Suddenly, I am a gourmet chef that needs to cook with the most expensive line of cookware? The entire thing is a joke. Seriously. We should all be registering for paper towels, mops and brooms, chips and salsa, boxed wine, duct tape, and couples therapy. And God. More than the heart-shaped waffle maker — we really need to register for a relationship with God. Because no amount of paper towels can clean up the marital mess that I, personally, am capable of making. Also? I don't even eat waffles. No matter how cute the shape. And waffles don't save marriages. If they did, I'd eat them.

I am not too sure where I got the idea that marriage was all sunshine and rainbows. I certainly knew from my own childhood that husbands and wives fight, that husbands and wives yell, and that still, at the end of the day, husbands and wives can stay married. And yet, on our first honeymoon night in Rome, after having some sort of squabble that was probably born out of post wedding exhaustion, not understanding the man at the hotel front desk, and too much red wine, I fell into bed crying, convinced we had made a mistake. Because what couple fights on their honeymoon? Who cries after only two days of marriage? Right then and there, I declared our marriage doomed.

And I continued to make these false declarations for many

years to follow. Rather than see problems and conflicts as an opportunity to strengthen our bond, I listened to the lie that told me, *You deserve better,* that *Something is terribly wrong,* that *He will never change,* and that ultimately, *You will never be happy.* While God was somewhere there in the picture, he most definitely was not the focal point of the grim portrait I had painted. I kept him hidden somewhere in the background and chose to call on my clueless friends for advice and answers to my big life questions, rather than call on my *all-knowing God and Father,* and have a listen to what he might have to say to his beloved daughter.

But that's just the thing. Back then? Back then, I did not know I *was* his beloved daughter. I did not know that my husband was his beloved son. I did not know that our marriage was a sacred sacrament, a giving of our very selves to one another, an outward sign of God's love for us to the entire world. That because we are sinners, and because we are human, it would be messy at times. It would be painful at times. It would be uncomfortable at times. But it would still be beautiful. I did not know that love was not a feeling, but rather a choice — a choice that I had vowed to make each and every morning of each and every day for the rest of our married lives. I did not know that it was not my husband's job to fulfill me, and that when you put your hope in another human being, you are destined to be let down. I did not know any of this, because I did not know God. You see, I had cast God in the smallest role possible for the greatest show of my life. I mean, he wasn't even a supporting role. He wasn't even in the chorus. He was a tree. Maybe even an *understudy* to the tree. That's how small. And God? God is not small. God is big. God is powerful. God is the duct tape that holds a marriage together. When I stood on that altar and spoke those vows, I had no idea that on that day, I was not entering into a marriage of two, but I was supposed to be entering into a marriage of three. Me, my husband, and God. Those vows I spoke? Those were not meant to be spoken. They were meant to be prayed.

I know there are people who will disagree with me. I

know there are people who do not believe in God and will say that they are perfectly happy in their marriage without him. Maybe they are. Or maybe the other shoe has simply not fallen yet. I am not saying we ought to be going through our marriages waiting for the other shoe to drop. I just know from forty-seven years of life that *shoes will drop* — and the times they dropped when I had Jesus way back, stage left, as a tree, those shoes fell hard. So hard, in fact, that those whispers telling me I deserved a better life than this, that things will never change, were all I could hear. And I believed them. And once you believe a lie, small wounds grow bigger, fractures break deeper, and the desire to throw away what looks unfixable is greater than the reality of the hope promised to us. There is hope that no matter the trial, God always provides a way out; that no matter the sorrow, there will be joy. That perseverance and endurance through the trial is what builds character. Sweet friend, we must persevere.

My husband and I have battled many storms together. And I want to point out that some storms — the violent ones, the ones that are unsafe, the ones that chip away at your soul and tell you that you are worthless — those are not to be weathered out alone. Some situations do require outside intervention, in addition to trust in God. There are times you need to get out and seek shelter, for your own safety, and that is the right thing to do. But I think this current throw-away culture we live in — this world of *Just do what makes you happy*, and *You are in control of your life*, and *Why should I have to settle?* — has us fooled.

People and circumstances are not what make us happy. We are not in control of our lives, no matter what anybody tells you. Good relationships will always demand sacrifice, and sacrifice does not, by the way, mean you are weak, or a pushover, or a doormat. It means you love; that you are willing to put others before yourself because of great love. The greatest love of all is not learning to love yourself, even though Whitney Houston told you so. Such a stupid line. Stop singing it. It is in the learning to love others more than you love yourself, in putting others before yourself, that you find true happiness. I think many of us have become so easily convinced that a bump in the road, or an unfamiliar detour, any sign of discomfort or uncertainty, is an indication that we need to lose our passenger, turn the car around, and find a better, smoother route. But the truth is God is calling us to take those roads on. He is calling us to drive these unfamiliar and unexpected highways together, trusting that he will guide us, trusting we will arrive at our destination safe and sound. But that requires putting Jesus in the driver's seat. Yes, go ahead and sing Carrie Underwood's "Jesus, Take the Wheel." I give you permission to sing that song.

You know, I have always said that I have never been improved by an easy time. And the same goes for marriage. Sure, my husband and I can sit on the couch with a bottle of wine and reminisce about the great experiences, the happy moments, those memories of clear-sky days and smooth sailing. But those conversations are not the ones that tighten our bond. Those stories are not the ones that strengthen and secure. It is the story of illness, the story of hurt, the story of bankruptcy, the story of misunderstanding, the story of tragedy, the story of trauma, the story of loss, the story of hard decisions, the story of pain, the story of sacrifice ... these are the stories that, like a drawstring bag, pull tight on the chords, close the gap, and bring us in closer. Because these stories? These stories, when lived out in faith, when endured to the end, always lead to God's mercy — and God's mercy always leads to forgiveness; and forgiveness always leads to healing; and healing always leads to wholeness. Then suddenly the "me" becomes "we," and the "I" becomes "you," and God is no longer an understudy tree, but center stage, the leading role, without whom the show could not go on.

So I just have to share that, between the time I sat down to write this and a day later when I finished up, my husband went out and bought me new slippers. The duct tape made this awful, squishy sound on the hardwood floor every time I took a step. Plus, I looked homeless. That (and his desire to keep me warm) was his motivation. They are a completely different style — a tan, shearling slip-on as opposed to the gray knit, boot-like slippers I wore down to nothing, and they are great. But I have yet to throw the other pair away. I am sure I will. But not just yet. Because I like the reminder. I *need* the reminder, that even when soles appear to be falling off in pieces, and thread, once knitted and beautiful, starts to pull apart, there is still hope. There can still be restoration. Don't throw something good away because it requires mending. Even broken things are still good. Even in broken things, hope finds a way. Real love is well worn. And God, like duct tape, wants to hold us together; to wrap himself around us, closing the holes, mending our souls, keeping us warm from the cold, hard ground.

BATTLE PLAN

If God has been taken out of your marriage, it is time to put him back in. My whole perspective on marriage changed when I read Saint Thomas Aquinas's definition of love: to consistently will and choose the good of the other. To desire the greater good for your beloved. Then it dawned on me: he is talking about heaven. Do you think about your marriage that way? Do you realize that it is your job to love your husband to heaven, and his job to love you to heaven? Pray with this definition of love and throw away the world's distorted view of love and marriage.

WEAPON OF CHOICE

I am torn on this one. I want you to put on the Breastplate of Righteousness to be sure that fragile heart of yours is protected. But I also really want you to break out the Shield of Faith, to "quench all the flaming darts of the Evil One." And when you think about it, the shield of faith isn't something you put on, it is something you hold up to protect yourself in all circumstances. It is strong enough and big enough to cover you, your husband, and your marriage. And you know what, marriage is so important I am going to go ahead and say, break out the Breastplate of Righteousness *and* the Shield of Faith!

Chapter 5

THE "WHAT IS MY PURPOSE?" BATTLE

"For I know the plans I have for you, says the LORD, plans for your welfare and not for evil, to give you a future and a hope."
— JEREMIAH 29:11

When I was about five years old, I dreamed of growing up and becoming a can of tuna. Seriously. Why? Because I loved tuna. I loved tuna so much, I wanted to be it. Made total sense to me at the time.

When I was eighteen years old, I went off to college to study musical theatre. I had high hopes of becoming a huge Broadway star, which may or may not have been as unrealistic as the can of tuna dream. However, I had experienced such great success in my small pond back home, that unlike the tuna dream, starring on Broadway seemed entirely possible. Besides, it was the only dream I had. It was who I believed I was, my sole purpose in life. I even gave out autographs (that nobody asked for) at our local Mexican restaurant on Friday nights. I was that kind of kid. So, yeah. This plan had to work.

Only, it didn't.

It didn't take long for this musical theatre major to recognize that I was no longer the big (tuna) fish in the sea. Every single person there was the big fish from their small pond. My first and only college play audition resulted in "don't call us, we'll call you." The sting of rejection hurt so badly that I quit on my dream altogether, just to be certain I would never feel that awful ever again. This way of self-protecting was not the best coping skill, but sadly, it was the only tool in my toolbox. I steered myself clear of future auditions gone wrong, but … now what? Nearly my whole life, my entire reason for existence as I knew it, was built upon this dream. This was my purpose, and now it was gone — and I was too old to fall back on the tuna plan. I was lost.

You see, this is what happens when we base our purpose on our success, when we believe our identity is wrapped up in what we do. Because let's be honest. At one point or another in life, we are all going to march out onto the battlefield and fail. Life is a series of battles, and not everyone walks off victorious. We will mess up, break up, be uninvited, lose the job, face rejection, not get the role. We may even get married, make our new husband a bowl of oatmeal for breakfast that he mistakes for a bowl of cement, and he'll never let us forget it — twenty-one years later, we will still be afraid to make our husband oatmeal because clearly, we are the worst oatmeal maker on the face of the earth, which can only mean one thing. We are horrible wives. (Or maybe that's just me?)

So, we need to build our worth and purpose upon something a little more solid (like my oatmeal). We need to define who we are in something other than starring roles (or good oatmeal-making skills). But I did not know that back then. I believed that what you do is who you are. When my own plan began to crumble (because who knew that God had a plan for me, as well?), so did my sense of purpose. After all, if what you do is who you are, and I was doing nothing, well then, that could only mean one thing: I was nothing.

When you feel worthless, all sorts of distorted feelings quickly move in, making themselves very much at home and leaving you feeling hopelessly stuck. And oh, sweet friend, if you have ever felt stuck, you know how dangerous a place this can be. Why? Because when we are stuck, we cannot move. We are perfect prey, and this is where the enemy loves us to be. It is the place where we set hope aside and grip fear with two hands. Before we know it, this little space we make slowly grows bigger and bigger, eventually inviting depression and despair to the party, creating the perfect battleground for the enemy of our soul. Why so perfect? Because we have just entered into enemy territory, completely unarmed, totally unprepared, unable to fight back.

I was certainly unarmed and unprepared in college. A cradle Catholic who knew about God, I never got to know God personally. His voice to me was ujnrecognizable because I only talked at him, not with him. I was good at barking off my list of orders, letting him know what I needed him to do for me, but I never stayed quiet long enough to see if he had anything to say back. But the enemy? Although I was unaware of it, I listened to him. I was in relationship with him. I had conversations with him. You see, unlike Jesus, who is a gentleman who lovingly waits at the door of my heart to be invited in, the devil is cunning and, well, kind of a jerk. He doesn't wait for an invitation, he looks for an opportunity. He was always lurking and prowling, circling like a lion, until he saw a small enough crack to slither on through. And once in, he whispered things in my ear: *Give up, you can't do this. You have no purpose. You failed. You do not belong here. Your life is meaningless. You have nothing. You are nothing. And by the way, you are fat.* These lies came at me like sharp arrows at full speed, piercing my heart, wounding my soul, and taking me out at the knees. And the worst part of all? I believed they were true. So deep in the battle, I quit musical theatre and majored in a raging eating disorder instead. Which by the way, if you happen to be considering starvation as your major, most colleges do not give credit for it, and buying into the meal plan is an enormous financial waste. I suggest you save your money for therapy instead.

Years later the battle continued to rage on, and my lack of purpose reached an all-time high. We had just moved across the country, left all of our friends, there was no money in the bank. (When I say no money, I do not mean we had a little money, I actually mean the balance was zero.) I was poorly wrangling four kids under the age of eleven, and the stress of it all had put our already strained marriage on life support. I remember standing at the kitchen sink, the usual pile of dirty dishes and cups before me, while some hideous cartoon blared in my ears from the next room. And standing alone, staring out the window with tear-stained cheeks, I recall thinking to myself, "Is this it? How on earth did I get here? What the heck is my purpose? Do I even have a purpose?"

You see, after the can of tuna and Broadway star dream didn't pan out (I know, weird), and I began eating again, I was content to live a simple life as wife and mother. Only, I was determined to be an always-super-happy wife and the-most-perfect mother who would raise a beautiful family with absolutely no problems. You know, like the ones in the Sunny D commercials. As the hot water ran, and the TV continued to play louder than sin, there was no denying that right there, in that very moment, I was anything *but* happy. My family was far from perfect. I was not feeling like a good, devoted wife. I was not feeling like a patient and loving mother. I felt like a giant loser who had failed at everything I was supposed to be. Now in the past, when I failed, be it at an audition or making oatmeal, my coping skills kicked right into action: run away, never try it again, don't make the stinking oatmeal. But it is much easier to run away from oatmeal than it is to run from your husband. It is a whole lot easier to run away from a dream than your children. (Believe me, I tried, but they always found me.) I had never felt more stuck, more alone, more purposeless in my entire life.

Maybe you have felt like this, too. Maybe you feel like this now. If so, I want you to listen up. That discouragement and despair you feel? That awful frustration and growing ache that tells you your life has no purpose? That cunning voice that whispers *You are alone, You have nothing,* and *You will feel like this forever?* None of that comes from God. Those subtle whispers that convince you of your worthlessness in your marriage, home, workplace, on this earth, are arrows of lies thrown directly at you by the father of lies. Most likely, he has been working on you for years. He certainly worked on me, knowing exactly what buttons to push, where I was weakest, pinpointing my most vulnerable places. He knows yours, too. He aims directly at these tender places, so that we not only fall down but stay down.

The questions we need to be asking ourselves are: How do I protect myself from these arrows? How do I shield myself from believing these lies when they do not even look like lies, when I am so convinced that they are true? How do I arm myself for battle when I often have no idea that I am even in battle?

First of all, let's start with this. We are always in battle. Never assume you are not. The moment you wake up, before you get out of bed, you, my sweet friend, are in battle. Before checking your phone or brushing your teeth or even looking at another person, know that the battle is on. Second of all, the only way to know a lie is to know the truth better. So third of all, get to know truth. The truth about you. The truth about your purpose. The truth about God.

The day I decided to open my Bible and read it was the day my life changed forever, and I do not say this lightly. Huge game-changer. For too long I went about life thinking I needed to prove my worth, believing my purpose was wrapped up in personal achievements. But God tells us differently. He tells us that he knew us before we were born, that he knit us in our mother's womb, that his plan for us is good. He calls us, his precious daughters, by name. He promises never to abandon us, always to help us, never to leave us alone. He tells us we are strong, clothed in dignity, and that we are worth more than five sparrows. He says we are beautiful like the dove, fragrant and lovely, and that we matter, not because of anything we have done or will ever do, but simply because we are his.

Our purpose was never meant to be something we needed to strive for or to prove. Nor is it something to be measured in earthly success. Our purpose is so much less complicated than we make it. God created you and he created me so that we would know and love and serve him. Remember, he died for us while we were still sinners, not while we were superstars. He came down to earth and became human because he wants us to live with him in heaven forever. We are worthy not because of anything we do, but simply because he loves us. We are his beloved. What more proof of purpose do we need?

I would love to tell you that this battle of mine has ended, but unfortunately, I'm still a hot mess from time to time and fall into the same traps. What can I say? Believing that my purpose is not something that is up to me to earn and prove remains a difficult task for me. It is still a battle for me to believe the truth that my identity is not about who I am, but *whose* I am. The enemy knows this. He knows this and he waits until I am vulnerable to make his attack. Only there's a difference now. I am prepared for the fight. How? Well, simply knowing I am in battle is half the battle! I have also traded in my pathetic coping skill (running away and never trying again) for the armor of God, which has made all the difference.

Through Scripture, I am intentionally getting to know this Father of mine who calls me beloved, who gave up his Son for me. Armed with his Word, I no longer show up on the frontline unprepared. So, if you find yourself staring out the kitchen window, your head filled with whispers and lies, wondering if you have any purpose, do this please, would you? Walk away. Walk away from the window, from the whispers, from the lies. Shut down the conversation with the one who aims to destroy you. Then run. Run to Jesus, sweet friend. Grab your Bible and marinate your weary soul in the truth. Read this great love story written about you, and for you. Then show up to battle with him. Bring your Father to the fight. His love alone will defend you.

BATTLE PLAN

Start reading Scripture, and if you already read Scripture, read more! Find a Bible study or an online sisterhood community. Read a spiritual book. Surround yourself with faith-filled friends and saturate yourself in truth.

WEAPON OF CHOICE

The Sword of the Spirit. The Word of God is the weapon that will cut away at the lies about who you are and reveal the truth about whose you are. Reach for this sword and ask God to reveal to you the truths you need to catch the enemy before he catches you. Pray with Isaiah 49:15–16. "Can a woman forget her sucking child, that she should have no compassion on the son of her womb? Even these may forget, yet I will not forget you. Behold, I have graven you on the palms of my hands; your walls are continually before me."

Chapter 6

THE BATTLE OF FINDING REST IN THE MESS

"Blessed be the LORD, my rock,
who trains my hands for war,
and my fingers for battle."
— PSALM 144:1

I rolled my eyes at God this morning. Come to think of it, I roll my eyes a lot, and not just at him, at everyone. When I was a kid I remember my mom telling me that if I rolled my eyes anymore, they were going to roll right out of my head. So I suppose it's been a bad habit for a long while now and probably not my best defense in winning the daily battle.

I wonder if Jesus ever rolled his eyes.

Yeah. Probably not.

There is just so much mess. This life of mine, and maybe yours too, gets so burdened with filthy garbage and heavy baggage. I don't know about you, but I am kind of tired of it all. I just want to clean it all up and throw it away and sit down and rest. But it feels impossible, doesn't it? There is so much unrest in this life, isn't there? And when I am not careful, which is all too often, this unrest and restlessness leads me to some serious battling in my heart — a battle for peace when life is in pieces.

I rolled my eyes at God this morning because, after jumping into Scripture in the hopes of finding an answer, any answer, to whatever it was that was causing me my current unrest, I doubted the Word that I read. So I rolled my eyes. At Scripture. At his promise. As if what I was reading was not the truth but some useless mumbo-jumbo that was a waste of my time. Because I am not new to this idea of life as a daily battle, I am smart enough to understand that perhaps this eye rolling, this doubting, this unrest — perhaps there is an enemy behind it. And I'll bet this enemy rolls his hairy eyes at God more than I do. In fact, I'll bet it is his scheming hands that start my own eyes spinning, and I'm pretty sure he gets a kick out of my calling sacred Scripture mumbo jumbo. Good grief, I have a long way to go.

Are you curious what I read that warranted my eye roll? In my own words, I read that if I come to Christ and bring him my mess, he will give me the rest I desperately need. And it is not so much the *"Come to me"* or the *"Bring me your burdens"* that I doubted. It was the promise of *"You will find rest."* Because lately? Lately, I have been hard pressed to find this rest. And I swear (yes, I know I should not swear, but I am a sinner and can't help it and so yeah … I swear), it is not for my lack of searching. Or trying. Or seeking out. Or coming to him with my dumpster fire of a life. I am giving it my spiritual all here. I want nothing more than to find rest in my mess.

Or do I?

I recently spent five days in Florida for my daughter's National Cheer Competition. It was hard to leave a family and a home and an enormous pile of work — a life that truly feels overburdened to the point of slow, bone-crushing death — just weeks before Christmas. In God's true fashion, the timing could not have been worse. I was encouraged by family and friends to enjoy the time away from the mess that feels like hands wrapped tight around my neck; to treat this like a well-deserved vacation. To enjoy the warmth. So I packed my bathing suit despite that being its own kind of horror and hideous battle, and off I went to rest in the hot sun.

It was exhausting. And cold. Yup. An unusual cold front hit Florida the day we arrived. There was zero warmth. So I ask, to what end, Lord? To what end?

Then I came home to even colder. To piles of laundry, filthy floors, and a mountain of untouched work that was growing on my desk like the weeds in my mind. To a mother in the hospital. To an important appointment on the calendar that I had completely forgotten about. The mess I left got messier. The burden got heavier. On top of all that, there was snow.

I did not feel rested.

I had found no rest.

I roll my eyes, and I continue to roll my eyes, because I cannot help but think to myself, *I do come to you, Lord!* In fact, I will go as far as to say that I run to him quite often. I bring him my burdens and I lay them all down, so will somebody please tell me, where is that rest he promises? Because clearly, I am not looking in the right places. I sit in my pool of doubt, and I question God, and by question, I mean I sort of yell at him, and I stop praying and I start demanding. *"TAKE THIS FREAKING MESS AWAY AND GIVE ME THAT STINKING REST."* Which, by the way, is not a direct quote from the Bible, in case you were wondering.

Because the truth is, I do not want his help to make this burden light.

I do not want to find rest in the mess.

I want him to take this burden away.

I want him to clean up the mess completely.

I just want it gone.

It is hard to learn this. It is hard to trust. It is hard to love the cross. It is hard to accept that he is *willing* whatever it is we are carrying that makes us feel weary and faint. Why can't he just take the burden away? If he loved us, he would do this, right? He would take the pain away. This is what the enemy wants us to believe. This is what the battle is really about. Can I trust a God who promises me rest and help but continues to keep me in the center of disaster? Is it possible to pick up my cross every day and follow him when what I really want to do is throw my cross out the window and go back to sleep? Oh man, how the devil delights in this thought: to lose the cross.

And we do this. *I* do this. And I see loved ones doing this. We do not want to accept the cross.

Not his.

Not ours.

We do not want help from anyone. Especially help from him, who wills this. Especially if this help is not an immediate fix. We do not want to accept this present trial, to accept this illness, to accept this financial burden, to accept whatever the heck it is we have strapped to our backs and wrapped around our necks completely exhausting us, and we do not want to reach out for help in carrying it.

WE JUST WANT IT GONE.

But that is not what he says to us, does he? He does not say, "Come to me and I will make this all go away." He says, "Come to me, and I will give you rest."

Unlike the father of lies and the prince of this fallen world, who convinces us that we need to get rid of anything remotely uncomfortable or unpleasant so we can be happy, Jesus claims that even with this burden, we can find rest. Even in the midst of sorrow, we can have joy. Even in the eye of the storm, we can find peace. Just come to him. *Even with.*

Back to this morning. Soon after I roll my eyes at Jesus, this Father of mine, who puts up with so much doubt from me, his precious and beloved eye-rolling daughter, pulls a memory from just days ago to the front of my chaos-filled mind. The memory of sneaking away from a hotel filled with cheer moms and daughters, stress and drama, false idols and competitive glares, to a beautiful church I had found online, just six miles away. He reminds me of how powerful that hour in his house was, how my friend and I both sobbed after receiving the Eucharist, and we did not know why. He reminds me of how nothing in my life had changed during that hour. Not the mess at the hotel and not the mess back at home. It was all still there. Yet, it had hit me like a ton of bricks as I knelt before him in that place: THIS is the only place I need to be. THIS is home. THIS is where I find rest.

My daughter looked at me halfway through Mass and said, "Mom, this is just like we do at church at home," and there it was … the rest. So I praised God for the Catholic Mass, and I thanked him for the universal Church, and I gave him all the glory for the unspeakable beauty that I found myself melting into, not wanting to leave. At last, in the midst of my mess, at the foot of the cross, I had found rest.

The temptation to put what has gone awry in perfect order is all too real and often necessary, but I think the mess has its place. I also think we need to stay alert and be aware when the mess around us begins to irritate and frustrate us, leading us into situations and emotions that are less than holy. I can always tell when my husband is mad at me because he starts cleaning. Angrily. I do this too. If you ever see me scrubbing my kitchen counters like an insane woman while yelling at my kids to pick up their socks and for once could they help with the dishes because why on earth we have thirty-four half-filled water glasses on the kitchen counter is beyond me … well, most likely someone has just pissed me off. While we may end up with a cleaner home, and a kitchen island that no longer looks like a frat house the morning after a party, nothing inside of us has changed. While we may stand in the center of a sockless family room, that unrest that dirties up our soul is still there. A clean toilet, as desirable as it may be, does not bring lasting rest. The only One who truly cleans up the mess (the mess that matters) is God.

And yes, he often allows us to sit in the mess for way longer than we care to. But we have to remember something here that the devil wants us to forget. He is GOD. He really does know so much more than we do, and he truly has our backs. He is our shield, our stronghold and our deliverer, and the battle is his. He's got this. So when Psalm 144 says, "Blessed be the Lord, my rock, who trains my hands for war, and my fingers for battle," perhaps this mess he lets us linger in is not because he thrives on torturing us, but maybe this messy season is an important part of our training for battle. Maybe this is how he conditions and strengthens us and builds up our trust, so when we run out into battle we are prepared soldiers of Christ. Just like the Bible story about the Karate Kid. Oh, wait. That was the movie with Ralph Maccio. I think I mean the story of David fighting the Philistines with just a slingshot and stone. But you know what I mean, right? The training might make no sense. And it will probably hurt, too. And it will absolutely require a trust in the One giving us the commands. But in the end, David overcame the Philistines. Just as the Karate Kid won the tournament. And don't even cry "spoiler alert" here, because this movie was made like four million years ago, and if you haven't seen it, I mean, honestly, where have you been?

Sweet friend, when life is a mess, the answer to finding rest is not cleaning it all up, but rather learning how to sit in it and still feel at peace. His presence, when we actively seek it out, without rolling our eyes, truly is the rest we need. This rest does not come from ridding ourselves of our burdens, but from allowing God to share in carrying the load. It goes against every human instinct I have: the instinct to solve every problem on my own, to carry all burdens by my own strength, to just drop it all on the side of the road and run away when the journey and the wait is just too long. This is why abiding in him is really a matter of life and death; why visiting him and being with him and kneeling before him daily is as essential as the air in our lungs and the coffee in our mugs. Because apart from him, there is no rest. Apart from him, we cannot win this battle.

He says *come to me*, and when I do (without rolling my eyes, without the spoiled-child demands) I am back home. I have found my soul rest. I thank him for not leaving this all up to me. I thank him for the mess that is training me for battle.

Suddenly, those hands that felt tight around my neck turn into the gentle warmth of his hand on the side of my cheek, and I do find rest. The mess is still there. The mess is still right here. But so is he.

BATTLE PLAN

Abiding in Christ and staying close to the cross is the only way to fight this battle. Forget the cross, and you can forget about victory. Pray daily, even when you feel like his Word is a bunch of mumbo-jumbo (and like your words are, too). When life feels extra messy and rest is hard to find, I drive myself to an empty church and walk up to the altar, drop to my knees, and literally put my hands out and say, "Here ya go. Take it." Sometimes I can kneel there before him for an hour; sometimes I literally walk in, lay it down, and walk out. Try this today. Because there is no place on earth that offers us better rest than the foot of the cross.

WEAPON OF CHOICE

This is a job for the Belt of Truth. Wrap yourself up in it and believe and trust in his promise.

Chapter 7

THE "IF ONLY I HAD THIS, LIFE WOULD BE PERFECT" BATTLE

"Wait for the Lord;
be strong, and let your heart take courage;
yes, wait for the Lord!"
— PSALM 27:14

I am truly in awe of those in this generation who "get it." You know the ones I am talking about. Those enthusiastic, on fire, youth ministry kids who grasp the truth, who understand that love, and peace, and happiness, have nothing to do with what they have, but everything to do with who has them. I am forty-seven years old, and I still battle with this truth. To this day, I catch myself praying for that quick fix, that easy solution, that simple purchase that will make all the pain, all the sorrow, all the discontent and disappointment go away.

And why not? I mean, if God is all-powerful, if God can move mountains, if God can not only part the waters but walk on them, too, then why not pray for that one thing to come through? I have read the Gospel stories. I know that he can heal. I know that he can restore sight to the blind with a simple touch. I know that he can raise people from the dead with a single word. So, why not? Why not pray for that one thing, that if only he would hand it on over to you, everything else would magically fall into place? And yeah, yeah, I know. God is not a magician. Whatever. I am not that stupid. I know that. But sometimes? Sometimes, I wish he was.

When I was a teenager, it was prayers for clear skin, a smaller nose, long legs, thin thighs, and straight, waist-length, blonde hair that occupied my heart and mind. In other words, I prayed to wake up and be Christie Brinkley. Because that is a prayer God will jump right on.

What can I say? Beauty was my idol. I worshipped the 1990s super model. Seriously. Remind me to tell you the story of how I followed Christy Turlington around the streets of the West Village in New York City for over an hour. Yeah. That wasn't creepy or anything.

I was just so convinced that if I looked beautiful by the world's standards, that life would be beautiful. Not everyone's life, of course. This wasn't about you. This was all about me. My vision and compassion did not stretch beyond my own warped reflection in the mirror. I wanted *my* life to be beautiful, and my desire for beauty did not stop at my personal appearance. As I have gotten older, I want everything around me to be beautiful. A beautiful home that is beautifully decorated, a beautiful family, beautiful birthday parties, a beautifully set holiday table, beautifully packed lunches in beautiful bento boxes, a beautiful husband, and beautiful pets — beautiful *everything*.

When I think about it, I realize that when I fell (and still fall) into this way of living, it was not truly living. Essentially, whenever I do this I'm *staging* my own life. As if there was a camera crew or real estate agent coming over to put a price on me, to determine my value, all based on how things look. Based on what I own. Based on how clean my bathrooms are. (If that were actually the case, if my value was seriously based on how clean my bathrooms were, well then, I'd be worth nothing. Absolutely nothing. Quite possibly, less than nothing, if that is even possible.) I really lived, and often continue to find myself living, with the ridiculous belief that if you could snap a photo of my day and it was worthy of a spread in *Vogue* magazine, I was good to go. I would be happy. Everything would be great. Which is fascinating, because if you did come over right now and snap a photo, *Vogue* would so not be an option. On the other hand, if you know of a magazine called *What a Freaking Mess* or *The Dog Pooped in the Hallway Again*, or *Good Grief, What's That Smell?* please share those publications with me. For sure, I could be on the cover, if not enjoying a full-page, full-color, center spread.

But you know, it is okay to desire beauty. We ought to be seeking out the beauty in our lives. We ought to be seeking out the beauty in other people's lives, too. But here is the thing. I wasn't really seeking *actual* beauty. I was seeking *surface* beauty. I was seeking the illusion of perfection. I was seeking outward appearances. I was seeking happiness in material things. In short, whether I knew it or not, I was seeking a foolproof way to avoid suffering, or a life void of anything remotely uncomfortable. It's as if I was applying a giant designer band-aid on anything in my life that threatened this idyllic way of living. I wanted a bandage that was big enough to stretch over my wounds, hide the pain, conceal the scars, and cover the gaping, aching holes that truly needed tending to.

The idea that if I only had *this* (this house, this man, this job, this marriage, this car, this degree, this haircut, this friend, this nose, this recognition, this newest technology), everything would be great, became the most believable yet unattainable lie ever sold to me. The idea that things could fulfill and people complete me became my way of life. And this works. It really does. *For about five minutes.* Then, when the band-aid doesn't stick anymore, and that wound is re-exposed, it is time to search for yet another thing, another idol, to keep our truest desire at bay and keep us slaves to false promises of happiness. I am convinced that this is why people constantly remodel their homes, change jobs, rearrange their furniture, and go for *just one more* plastic surgery procedure. Because, sweet friend, when we turn to things and our bodies and other human beings, expecting them to fix and fill whatever brokenness and emptiness we are dying from, the restlessness in our hearts only grows bigger and stronger, and we are left worse off than we were when we initially began.

Temporary is exactly how it sounds. *Temporary.* Not long-lasting. I suppose there are times when a temporary fix or solution works. Kind of like when I lost my only pair of reading glasses, which was a huge problem, considering I have gone completely blind in a matter of months, and I cannot see anything without them. (Seriously. If you live in my neighborhood, think twice about being on the road at the same time I am. Especially at night.) So, until I was able to pick up a new pair, I had to borrow my husband's readers. They were not feminine and pink and pretty, from the cute little gift shop in town, like my readers that came in an adorable linen case. These were old-man glasses. That came in a pack of three. From Costco. I looked ridiculous, but I was okay with that, because I understood that this fix was just temporary. They would do the job until I could get my own pair.

But losing my reading glasses, in the grand scheme of life, is really no big deal. We lose bigger things sometimes. We lose needed jobs. We lose loved ones. We lose our homes. We lose our dignity. We lose our minds. We lose all hope. We simply lose. When we feel *that* loss — when we can identify that what we are experiencing is a significant inner emptiness, and that if this emptiness is not filled with something fast, we might possibly die from the deep growl within — it is precisely then that we have an incredible opportunity. We can run out and buy ourselves a temporary fix, causing immediate relief, and numbing us from head to toe. Or … we can sit in this feeling … and wait. We can acknowledge our heart, tap into the pain, and understand that there is nothing this world can ever offer us to make this all go away. No addition on the house. No pair of shoes. No bottle of wine. No plastic surgery. No diet. No other human being. There is nothing we can buy or use that will ever be the answer. So we rest in this uncomfortable truth. We wait.

Yup.

We wait.

Don't we all love to wait?

Good grief, I think we are the most impatient generation this world has ever seen. Everything is instant. Our rice. Our popcorn. Our photographs. Our stories. Our favorite TV shows. Our dinners. Just throw your life into a silver pot, press ON, and in five minutes, everything you ever wanted will be all yours! No need to wait, ever! I think this is such a tragedy. Why? Well, first of all, it makes for a really unpleasant experience while waiting to check out at the grocery store. The huffing and puffing around me when the line is more than three people long is off-the-charts crazy. It takes everything inside of me to not pick up my box of tampons or jar of peanut butter and throw it at the heads of the people who need everyone around them to know that they have somewhere they must be. I mean honestly, people, everyone in the checkout line at Stop & Shop can't be a heart surgeon late for a transplant. Slow down. Pray a Rosary, or do an examination of your conscience, or pray for the poor cashier who has to deal with you.

Personally, I think there is great wonder in the waiting. I think there is beauty in the waiting. I think there is so much to be learned and to be gained and to be hoped for in the waiting. But waiting requires things of us that we are not so good at. Things like patience. Things like trust. Things like faith. Things like being quiet and still. Things like not having control. Things like feeling those feelings we have worked really hard to push away. I think we are terrified of these things. Especially that "being still" part. Because you know what happens when we sit still? Nothing. Nothing happens. When nothing happens, something else does. SomeONE else does. God happens.

God loves it when we stop fighting him and sit still. It allows him this sweet gap to step into, to search for and rescue us. He is so quiet, this sweet Savior of ours. He whispers ever so softly, and gently tugs at the corners of our hardened hearts. He points to those places and spaces we have been running from. He reveals that ugly, messy, festering wound we have been tirelessly concealing with band-aids that don't stick. Oh, how we hate this. First of all, who likes having anyone point out what's not working for us? But also, because we are smart cookies, we know that we have been running, avoiding, and working too hard at filling our lives with all the wrong things. We know that changing our ways and letting go of idols means feeling all sorts of things we do not ever want to have to feel and will most likely take us to places we really do not want to go.

But sweet friend, healing — true, inner, authentic healing — is never going to be instant. Trust me. I know. I have prayed for instant healing for four years now. Each morning I still wake up to a road of healing ahead. To still more bruises yet to be pointed out, pressed upon, and uncovered. Like you, I hate it. But there comes a point when the running is just too much. There comes a point when resting from the race is essential. It is always in this stillness, and in the hard waiting, that God slowly works on us. That God slowly works *in* us. It is in quiet surrender and humble recognition that we can finally unwrap the bandages, open wide the door of our hearts, and let our Healer in.

What helps me in my seasons of waiting it out in the pain is to recall the past seasons. I remember all the past circumstances that felt unending while going through them, but how they did, in fact, end. It helps to recall the times I grasped at the temporary fix, the quick purchase, the instant latest thing, the toxic relationship, the beauty procedure to numb the bad feelings, even if only for a moment. Because what I take away from both approaches is rather eye-opening. The instant? The quick? The magic? When I choose these, I learn nothing besides regret. Nothing changes. I am still me, untransformed. I am still me, unsatisfied. I am still me, unfulfilled. I am still me, with a heart of stone. But when I choose to wait it out? To sit still? To listen for God's voice? To feel? To allow his loving hand to rest upon my exposed wounds? When I make the hard choice, lessons are learned. Everything changes: I am no longer unsatisfied and unfulfilled.

Now I can look at life with an eternal perspective. I can ask myself, *What does this mean for my eternity?* rather than *How can I satisfy myself in this present moment?* When I do this, my heart of stone becomes fleshy and alive. What is born out of the pain is a beauty beyond anything I had ever imagined. What blossoms out of the trial is compassion and love for others who are also struggling to find purpose and meaning in their lives. You see, if we allow God to show up and do his thing, if we choose Christ alone and quit trying to control and piece together a life that *looks* good, everything might not be great — but everything will be grace.

Now listen up, because here is the honest and ugly truth. THIS IS HARD. I still do not always choose right. I still wish that Jesus was never nailed to that cross, but had remained on the ground instead, in a black tuxedo and top hat — one he pulls fluffy, white rabbits out of. He'd be such a good-looking magician, don't you think? But we really do know better. We really do know that he is so much greater than that. That he loves us too much to swoop in and say *abracadabra*, only to fly off leaving us, really, no different from how he found us. Because Jesus isn't like that. We must be careful to not reduce him to this quick fix, birthday party magician, who distracts us for an hour, fools us a little, and then moves on. Because when you truly encounter Jesus, guess what? You do not stay the same.

Isn't this what we are hopelessly in search of? A change? Isn't this why we color our hair, and buy new furniture, and change schools, and walk away from marriages, and move across the country, and make those impulsive decisions? Because we are in desperate need of something to change? Sweet friend, Jesus can change you. Jesus can change me. And if Jesus can change me, than good grief, he can change anybody. Maybe not instantly, but what truly good things happen in an instant? Your life is not a problem to fix, but an opportunity to grow in relationship with the One who knows why you are here — the One who created you for something beautiful, who never promised you a perfect life, but who does hold your perfect plan.

Maybe it would be good for us to remember this. Maybe it would be good to think about what idols we hold tight to, what things we grasp for to satisfy, what wells of unquenching waters we run to when we are dying of thirst. Then throw away your instant pot and break out the slow cooker. And then … just wait.

BATTLE PLAN

Are you in a season of waiting? Waiting for God to step into your life and clean it all up immediately? I am right there with you, and it is not easy. Let's choose to wait patiently — without rolling our eyes. Prayerfully list all the ways that God has showed up in the past. Tell him that you trust he will not leave you this way, and then thank him for all of the great things he has yet to do. He will not leave you to die in your mess. He hasn't yet, and he never will. If he does, I will die first. I promise.

WEAPON OF CHOICE

Let's stand firm against the tactics of the devil, with our feet shod "with the equipment of the gospel of peace." By putting on the Sandals of Peace, we stand our ground. We dig our heels in, and we proclaim truth in the face of the lie. We will not be shaken, we will not grow weary, we will not grow faint, and we will not feel like this forever. Keep your shoes on and stand tall and strong believing that God will lead you out of this mess into greener pastures. Confident that even in the midst of the battle, you will find rest.

Chapter 8

THE "TOO BUSY FOR GOD" BATTLE

"Commit your work to the LORD,
and your plans will be established."
— PROVERBS 16:3

My family just moved. This move marks ten home relocations for us in just twenty years. We should have been Nomads. Or a military family. Or gangsters on the run. You'd think we would have it down by now, but we don't. Every move we still get overwhelmed by all of our stuff, distracted by all of the necessary details of changing the mailing address and hooking up the Internet. We have four children, so hooking up the Internet is like supplying them with oxygen. Do it, or they die.

Moving your entire life is not for the wimpy, and doing it with children and an assortment of furry things with four legs who thrive on escaping and running through the neighborhood while foaming at the mouth makes it all the more difficult. On top of the craziness of uprooting and replanting, there is still that thing that continues to happen — LIFE. Laundry to do, kids to care for, jobs to go to, dogs to walk, dinner to make (Lord, have mercy on me). As I pack away items, and toss out those things not making the cut, something very important usually, and unfortunately, gets packed away until "the dust settles," until I have the time. Something that should be left out of the packing, kept close, and taken with me everywhere, never to be stored or tossed away.

God.

Quiet and intentional time with my Lord gets put in a box and promised to be reopened when things are not so crazy busy. He understands, I am sure. He sees how busy I am. It's not like I am skipping Mass on Sunday, right? I mean, it is true, I am not making it to my usual daily Mass, but daily Mass is not *required* of me, right? I am still checking off my obligation box, so it's all good.

Or is it? We all know how fruitful those relationships that feel like nothing but an obligation are, right?

When the routine is off, and your best daily habits are easily forgotten because there are too many things that you need to do; when you can't recall where you packed your shoes so you are wearing only winter boots and slippers, and you have no idea where the heck you packed your razor, which explains why the hair on your legs is longer than the hair on your head, confusion sets in and priorities shift. Because honestly? I have to find that razor. It is the number one priority. Forget the hairy legs, you should see my beard. It is impressive.

The battle of crazy busy is widespread and not limited to those times we are just moving and replanting our homes. Because let's be honest. *We are always moving.* We are always on the go, running errands, driving kids, going to work, volunteering, cramming in meetings, going to the gym (you, not me), picking up take-out because we hate to cook (and yes, by "we" I mean me). We are always on the move and we live by the mantra, "I am crazy busy." As if crazy busy means crazy productive, or crazy important, or crazy successful. We are so off the mark, aren't we? Because crazy anything is just crazy.

As far as I know, crazy is not a good thing. Why do we believe that it is? Why would I refer to this as a battle?

I think most of us believe that the devil comes at us fast and furious and wreaks all sorts of obvious chaos when we are under attack. But that is a lie. In fact, the enemy is incredibly smooth and subtle. He's crafty, as described in Genesis 3:1, and I don't mean crafty in a Joanna Gaines shiplap kind of way. I mean crafty as in a shrewd, cunning serpent. He goes about destruction in a most careful and calculated manner with an impressive amount of patience. He's so under the radar that he has us opening doors and cracking the windows to let him in, and we have no idea. These doors and windows we are willingly opening are the ones that lead directly to our hearts, the very place inside of us that should be reserved for God and God alone. But if we are being honest, can we truly say that God is first in our hearts? If we were to really sit down and unpack our hearts, would we easily find God there, or would he be buried beneath all of those distractions? Is God occupying our hearts, or are our jobs, errands, stresses, worries, exercise classes, and all of those other things that are keeping us so crazy busy, occupying our hearts? An easy way to figure out where your heart is: look at your calendar. Is God anywhere on it?

My favorite C. S. Lewis quote is from *The Screwtape Letters*, a series of letters from the senior Demon Screwtape to his nephew Wormwood, who is a Junior Tempter. Screwtape says this: "It is funny how mortals always picture us as putting things into their minds: in reality our best work is done by keeping things out." Think about that and then ask yourself what is being removed from your mind that would make the enemy happy.

What am I not allowing in because I am just too distracted by too many other things? If you do this, and if you do this honestly, I bet that as much as you love the Lord and as much as you wish to follow him and allow him to lead every move of every day, he is not always top priority. My guess is he is not the only occupant that rests in the inn of your heart. My guess is that God is way down there on your priority list, somewhere after yoga class and posting that carefully filtered picture of that really amazing kale salad you had for lunch. When Christ drops in the rankings, the devil has just gained a stronghold. Because, sweet friend, if God is not number one in our hearts, something else is. This is the enemy's targeted entry point. And he doesn't knock or wait for an invitation. He just slithers on in.

One of the ways I am able to recognize when I am allowing busyness to remove Christ from my heart is when I start to rationalize my behavior and make excuses for putting God on the back burner. When I look at my calendar and plan it all out, as if I am actually the one in control of my life, promising God as I do my children, "Hang on one more minute! I will be right there!"

What goes on in my mind sounds a lot like this:

If I can just get through this situation, then things will fall into place, and I will have time to pray again.

If I can just get this one thing done and out of the way, then I will be able to think straight and then I can get back to daily Mass.

If I can just battle through this week, then I will have that time to rest with Lord.

These are my crazy busy thoughts. Guess what? They are not just crazy, they are also stupid. I will tell you why. Because there is always something. ALWAYS.

No matter how many things we get through, get done, battle through, guess what? There will be something else around the corner waiting. Our lives are a never-ending thread of things needing to be done. But we stay on this treadmill of "go and do," and all the time we are wondering why we haven't moved ahead. Why we still feel overwhelmed by things and stuff and alarms on our phones. We cross items off lists only to add more, so we grab coffee on the run and pour that third glass of wine as we fall into bed, because good grief, why can't we keep up? I'll tell you why. Because we have just registered ourselves in a race that has no finish line. And not only is there no finish line, but the one who is coaching us and cheering us on — telling us to keep on running, don't stop and rest, just go, go, go until we collapse — has no intention of allowing us to catch our breath. We have no shot at winning, ever.

Shocking that we have anxious hearts, isn't it?

Looking ahead and planning for the future can be fun, if there is something fun to look forward to. Getting a brand new planner and filling it all up gives us this weird sense of accomplishment, doesn't it? But as I get older, my looking ahead is usually born out of fear, worry, and dread ... and it robs me of the NOW. It distracts me from the present moment. These thoughts become a crowd that comes in and clouds my mind, blocks my heart, keeping me from living in the present. This looking ahead, needing to be in control, mapping out our every move and activity, is not the way to achieve peace in our day. A fully checked-off to do list is not our ticket to heaven. So, this life of yours? It is not actually yours. It belongs to God. Nowhere in the Bible can I find him saying, "Blessed are those who think everything is all up to them, because it is."

When we fall into this trap, thinking that it is all up to us, we enter the battlefield not only unarmed, but exhausted and probably starving, because there was no time to stop and eat, and we considered that latte at 2:00 p.m. our lunch. What an easy target a weary, hungry woman is! So, we take our place on the frontline, crawling instead of marching. Wounded before the first arrow flies by. Our rest has been replaced with stress. We are practically defeated before we've even begun to fight. But here is the thing. The battle has been raging on. The moment we eliminate God from our daily plan and choose to move forward without him, the attack has already begun. I have to believe that in today's world, where we wear our busyness like some sort of badge of honor, this is a most common area of attack. It is a deadly one. Because this, sweet friend, is when we start to believe that what we do is what we are, and if we do not accomplish everything, we are failures. This is when we believe that stopping to rest and adding time with God in our lives means we cannot possibly accomplish the demands of our everyday lives. So, he gets pushed farther and farther down the priority list, until one day, he is not on the list at all.

I used to live this way, you know. I used to think that stopping to pray or going to daily Mass was a ridiculous impossibility, not to mention a little selfish. I mean, sitting down in the afternoon with a cup of coffee and a devotional? When there is laundry to be done? and a sink full of dishes? and that stupid dinner I am supposed to make every single night of my life until I am dead? Isn't that being irresponsible, unproductive, and lazy? This is what I used to think. Because I believed that a life of crazy busy meant it was purposeful — that *I* was purposeful — and the thought of stopping and resting literally made my skin crawl. At first, my skin did crawl. Sitting on the couch and carving out intentional resting time with the Lord was super difficult. Every time I sat down to pray, I found my mind wandering to that to-do list. Even today, I can get on my knees with the desire to pray the Rosary, and by the third decade I realize I have just redecorated my living room and planned a grocery list in my mind. But I have learned that it's okay. When the crazy busy enters and tries to rob me of this precious time with the Lord, I simply ask him to forgive me, to please help bring my focus back to him and take it off that darling farm table Chip Gaines made from an old, rustic barn, that would look so good in my dining room.

Resting with God is not easy for us, is it? But I have learned that if I truly want to get things done, things that matter, this must become a daily habit. It took too many years of constantly looking ahead, just trying to survive barely enough until I could see that light at the end of the tunnel, to recognize that Jesus *is* the light. We can have the light even in the dark. We can feel the joy in the midst of the sorrow. We can live worry-free despite feeling "off track." We can rest in his arms despite the crazy busy.

Because the light at the end of the tunnel is nothing compared to the light of Christ that is here right now, in the middle of your busy and mess.

We must abide in Christ to win this battle. Because he holds our blueprint, and he knows exactly what we should be doing. No, worrying about the future and doing everything by our own strength is not on his list. You know what happens when we do this? when we make time for him? when we bring him our calendar and ask him what should stay and what should go? Life falls into place. Never forget: this awesome, almighty God of ours is a God who multiplies — who takes whatever small offering you have and leaves you with leftovers. Bring him your day, and he will give you more than enough time to get it all done. The day I went from the crazy busy to crazy for Jesus was the day this marathon I am running became possible to win.

How, you might ask? How do I abide in Christ when I am so completely depleted? when the demands on me are just too much? when the whole entire world depends on me, and I do not even have the time to shave the beard on my chin? (Not just my chin, but my neck! In all of this running around, did I mention that I discovered three white hairs that are jutting out of my neck? I look like a freaking cactus! I have no time to pray because I have to tweeze!) But there is time. There is plenty of time. Time to say a silent prayer before you get out of bed. Time to keep the holy name of Jesus on your lips throughout the day. Time to say thank you for every sip of your coffee, even when you spill it all over your desk when you sit down to work and you think to yourself, *Seriously, Lord?* Even then. There is time to do all of this (and still tweeze that unspeakable amount of hair that God must have thought was a real hoot when he created you — and by you, I mean me).

Another thing that has helped me greatly in this battle is intentionally seeking out connection. Connection to

real people. Face-to-face time with a friend I can talk to.
Someone who can sit across from me and speak truth and life
back into my anxious and weary heart. Finding this person
is key to your spiritual life and your stamina to press on in
the midst of a war. It certainly has been to mine. Someone
who is not out to fix you or judge you, but who can listen
and say "me too," is a gift from God. A sister in Christ who
prays over you might sound awkward and uncomfortable at
first, but I gotta say, it is the most beautiful treasure you will
find. But this is a gift and treasure we usually refuse because
we think we do not have the time to connect. Do not fall
into this trap. We need sister warriors. We need other daughters of Christ to stand with us on that frontline, shoulder to
shoulder, shielding us from the arrows aimed directly at our
hearts. Together, side by side, we become a shield wall. We
become stronger. We stand a much better chance of winning
the battle. We need to keep these people close, and we need
to make that coffee date with them now, not when the dust
settles, or next week, because we are just too crazy busy.
Not when we see the light at the end of the tunnel, because
did you ever consider that this meaningful relationship that
carries you through the tunnel just might be the guiding
light sent to you by Christ? (I will bet you a bag of chips and
a jar of salsa that you have a friend in mind right now who
you have been meaning to have coffee with … and you keep
saying *soon, when things aren't so busy.* Am I right? I *am* right. I
win. And FYI, I prefer multigrain chips. Thank you.)

I think we need to intentionally step out of the crazy busy
and rest with what matters, not with what we are convinced
needs to happen and can only happen if we do it because really,
it is all up to us, right? Amazing the mountains are still standing,
and quite honestly, aren't we the ones who keep those mountains
up there in the first place? Um, yeah. No, not us at all.

But what matters? I mean, really, ask yourself this now.
What truly matters to you? Here's my list:

- God
- My husband and marriage

- Our children
- Authentic friendships
- Leading other women to Christ

(Please notice that tweezing my entire body is not on the list.)

What is that thing — the thing that brings you easy, simple joy — that you are not doing because you are waiting until you have the time to do it? Stop whatever is getting in your way and just do it. The mountains will not crumble, I promise. Let's step out of the crazy busy today and choose to be crazy only for Jesus. Because I am thinking right now that this crazy busy we fall into becomes its own idol. I am thinking that crazy busy is what robs us of crazy love and contentment. Actually, now I am thinking that this crazy busy is what self-seeking death might be all about. We want to live today, don't we?

This battle can be won, you know, but we need to show up as warriors of Christ, not wounded of the world. So, make that coffee date, plan that rest, and set crazy busy aside. Put God back in your heart and make a promise to bring him your calendar every single morning, following only his lead. Guard your heart for all it is worth, and recognize when other occupants have pushed their way in. Then look up and thank the Lord for the mountains. Because, as I have discovered, no matter the dishes left in the sink, or the laundry still unfolded in piles, those mountains will still be standing. Better yet, I am still standing, too.

BATTLE PLAN

Bring your calendar to God every day. Ask him to show you those things he would like you to get done and those things that can wait. Ask him for protection over your heart, and the strength to keep him and his presence in the number one spot on your to-do list.

WEAPON OF CHOICE

This is a no-brainer. Put on your Breastplate of Righteousness and meditate on Proverbs 4:23. "Keep your heart with all vigilance, for from it flow the springs of life."

Chapter 9

THE "REALLY, GOD, *THIS* IS MY CALLING?" BATTLE

"And I heard the voice of the Lord, saying, 'Whom shall I send, and who will go for us?' Then I said, 'Here am I! Send me.'"
— ISAIAH 6:8

In 2017, I had the honor of emceeing a Catholic women's retreat, surrounded by my beautiful sisters in Christ, listening to the most incredible praise and worship music, witnessing so many lives experiencing a flooding of the Holy Spirit as they encountered Christ in an intimate and personal way. I was on cloud nine. It was like having a front row seat to a heart transformation, which is different than a front row seat to a heart transplant. I wouldn't want to see that. But a woman's heart softening and opening to the love of her heavenly Father? That I like to see.

That weekend was hands down one of the most beautiful and powerful moments of my entire life. It was as if everything I had done in my past, the good and the bad, all led up to such a time as this — this plan, carefully orchestrated by the hand of God. It was a "top of the mountain" moment for sure — and I don't know about you, but I much rather prefer hanging out at the top of the mountain to blindly wandering in the bitter valley. I think I am way more effective and can really express my love of the Lord to others so much better when I am placed up high on that mountain. Preferably with a spotlight (and maybe a glass of wine). Plus, and I am not sure why, I totally look skinnier up there, too. At least ten pounds thinner. I mean, honestly, if God really knew what was best for me, he would keep me up there, on top of that mountain. Rocking a size four.

If God really knew what was best for me. I am a piece of work, aren't I?

My dear girlfriends, whom I refer to as my "Marys and Marthas," gifted me with a pretty, rustic sign that weekend. On the sign is a verse adapted from chapter 4, verse 14, in the book of Esther: "Perhaps this is the moment for which you have been created." I proudly hung that sign up in my bedroom when I returned home, right in a spot that I can see always, right in a place that was certain to remind me of that mountaintop weekend, bringing back all sorts of good feelings and joyful memories. And I would kneel beneath it and whisper my prayer of thanks and praise, and think to myself, "Life has really come together for me, hasn't it? This writing and speaking and proclaiming the Lord to my sisters in Christ — this *is* what I was made for! This is my moment! I have found my calling! Thank you, Jesus, for threading and stitching up my messy life into this amazing tapestry of holiness! Keep me right here Lord … this is where I am meant to be! Now can you top me off please, because my wine glass is almost empty."

I'm such an idiot.

Not too many months after that glorious weekend, I found myself thrown into the deepest distress and unrest over one of my precious children. Severe suffering and a feeling of hopelessness and weariness hit me so hard that, if I am being honest, if given the choice to live or to die, I would have chosen death. Mothers are like that, right? We would give our very lives to ease our children's pain, wouldn't we? I would trade suffering with any one of my children at a moment's notice. I would take it all on so that they could be free and whole, healed and well. Except for head lice ... and pinworms. But other than that, no question about it, I'd take it. Make no mistake, I was not suicidal, although I know that whole choosing death thing sure sounds like it. When I found I was at the very bottom of myself, I was not contemplating how I could end my life so that I would not hurt anymore. I just wanted the pain to go away for my child. I needed it to go away for all of us. The thought of enduring it for one second more felt unbearable and impossible. I needed this circumstance to be wiped away because I did not have what was required to run this race. So I fell to my knees on my bedroom floor, and I wept out loud. I let God know that this thing he had placed on me? On my sweet child? It was just too much. I told him I was too small and weak for this. I reminded him of how afraid I am, how afraid I get, how he was calling me into the very waters that I knew for a fact would swallow and drown me. "I do not want this, Lord" was the only thing I could say. "You need to take this away" became my prayer.

Then I looked up and I saw that pretty, rustic sign. "Perhaps this is the moment for which you have been created." A light inside of me went on. The pain eased just enough, allowing me to lift up my eyes, to sit up straighter and stronger.

Like a beggar I held out my empty hands, looked to the heavens, and in all humility and trust I responded out loud to God's calling in the three words that bubbled up from my heart and into my mind: "HOLY CRAP. Really?" Because I heard his voice and because his call to me was all too loud and clear.

This, right here. The weeping mother on the floor praying and fighting for her child? *This* was the moment I was created for. Not the call I wanted at all.

Oh, the battle! When it comes to hearing God's call and

accepting it with joy, I am like the rope in a game of tug-of-war, with Satan on one side and Jesus on the other. The enemy tries to pull me close to him, away from Christ. He wants to keep me out of the light of hope and possibility, so he tugs me into the darkness of doubt and impossibility. He wants me to be afraid, to question God's plan for me, and to stay stuck in my fear. He wants me to believe that I am not big enough for God's calling, and that, really, the calling kinda sucks. Ultimately, he wants me to give up and surrender. With each hard pull, the lies flood my mind, and I start to believe that there is no way I can boldly step into the arena that God has called me into. NO WAY. Because this cannot possibly be what I was created for, and if it is, well then God doesn't know me at all, because how can any of this be for my good? How can any of this be for my child's good? Does God even own a dictionary? Does He even know what good means?

As I entertain these absurd thoughts, removing God from my mind and continuing to converse with the enemy of my soul, it is here that I drop my weapons and blindly walk straight into the raging battle. It is here that I decide I am not only ill-equipped to respond to God's call, but I am going to flat-out back away from it. Because God's call for me? So not happening. He can go ahead and give my call to someone else. You know, someone who thrives on unspeakable pain, heartbreak, and discouragement (and might as well throw in enjoys making dinner every night as well). See ya later, Lord … the devil and I are headed up that mountain in our skinny jeans. We might even stop for a latte on the way.

But we never quite make it there — and there's definitely no latte. Because you see, the enemy, like God, has a plan for us too. And it is pretty simple: to keep us from our Father's love. To reject him. To tune him out completely. To walk away convinced that what we plan for ourselves is going to be so much better than what he has planned for us. He wants us to settle for less than we were created for. He wants to keep us from transformation and spiritual growth because the last thing he wants is another female warrior of Christ. The enemy wants to keep us wounded and afraid, and his schemes are not just limited to us, but they spread out like a disease, infecting those we love. He goes after our hearts and everything they hold dear. He whispers to us that we can never win this battle, we can never fight strong, we can never possibly rise up to the call. But God is Sovereign. No matter the obstacle Satan puts between us, God is still bigger. He sees beyond the enemy lines, and he knows the battle plan before it was even created. God is our general in this war, and this is a fight he has already won. We may not understand why he is asking us to march into what feels excruciating and impossible, but we must never forget that wherever he calls us to go, he is there. He goes before us, and he will never leave us. We do not fight alone.

God is calling each one of us, personally and specifically. I think we have the habit of looking at the crowd around us and feeling like other people's callings are so much better than ours. I know I do. When the ground felt like it had dropped from beneath my feet, I couldn't believe what God was calling me to do. It was a moment when my faith was truly put to the test, and thank God he let me take a retest, because pretty sure I failed the first one. The reason I failed was because I didn't trust him. I didn't trust that I was the right one for the job. I didn't trust that doing what felt so incredibly wrong to me was a part of his careful and well thought out plan. At the end of the day, the truth is I didn't want to accept that *this* was my life. That *this* was my call. That *this* was the moment I was created for. I wanted to be created for easy and feel-good and skinny jeans. I wanted to be created for beautiful moments that came with applause and flowers and giant cups of coffee. I thought that was what a calling was all about. Each time God would call me into the center of his will, I, like a defiant toddler, would take one step farther away. I wanted to follow him, and I wanted to stay close, but I also really wanted my will over his. Because his will? It was too unpredictable. It was not what I had planned. It didn't fit into my idea of what my life was supposed to look or feel like. It was not only super hard, but it was also looking like it was going to super hurt. I don't know about you, but I don't like hurting.

Not all callings are difficult, and not all callings are painful, but let's be honest, some are. The difficult ones I have discovered are the ones we need to accept and pay good attention to, because in true Catholic form, they are the ones that transform us. The good times in our life are just that. Good times. But the trials we endure actually mold us and shape us into something better. Something bigger. Something so much more beautiful. I have always said that I have never been improved by an easy time, and it is true. The good stuff in our lives doesn't always look good. Chances are that the dirty and the ugly that bring forth beauty are not going to be something you want on your Pinterest board or sent out as your Christmas card. Although we should, because really, how much more interesting would that be than your family in matching red sweaters at a tree farm? But we would never do that. Because nobody wants to post their breakdown. The truth is, my sweet friend, without the breakdown, we can't have the breakthrough. And it is most likely the call to your cross that is where you will find your breakthrough.

It is always in the falling apart that we find the blessing. The call to that very mess, that illness, that loss, that tragedy, that hardship, that one thing you begged God not to send you … could it be that this is the good stuff? Could it be that what we see as problems to solve and remove are actually our best opportunities to live and to grow? I hate to say it, but I think so. Why? Well, my therapist told me. But also, because the call to hard places is the stuff that keeps us running to the foot of the cross. Think about it. When you have a great day, do a little shopping, grab a latte, have dinner and drinks with friends, get your nails done, do you drop to your knees when you get home, crying tears of joy and praising God for the amazingly easy day you just had? Because I don't. What gets me to that place of total surrender is when God's will steamrolls right over my will, when I have forgotten how to breathe on my own, when I have been called to do the impossible. When there is nowhere else to go but to my knees, and with my last bit of life I reach for my best weapon — my Rosary beads — and I pray like I have never prayed before. "Here I am, Lord. Tell me what I need to do. Show me how to answer this call."

When we do not want to accept the call, when we would rather run away from it than directly into it, we miss out on the opportunity to grow closer to him. We miss out on the incredible gift of standing beside our Blessed Mother, who is already there, who already knows and understands what it means to be called to something you do not fully understand but to do it anyway, because God has asked you to. Mary's calling was the original #blindside, yet she was addressed by the angel as "highly favored," and her cousin Elizabeth called her "the most blessed of all women." Although deeply disturbed by the message, she believed in the fulfillment of God's promise. When we do this, when we choose to believe, allowing the tug of Christ to pull us into what feels like it might literally kill us, we will be pleasantly surprised to learn that what appeared to be pulling us down was actually pulling us up. Up to our feet. Up to our cross. Up into his arms. Up into the blessing, with our heavenly Mother standing at our side. How do I know? Because I finally did it. I finally let go of my will and my fear, and I allowed myself to be pulled into the very place I begged God not to take me. And guess what? I am still alive.

I wish my calling was centered around shopping at Anthropologie and an endless supply of chips and salsa. Perhaps helping the poor. But seriously. I can't be the only one who sometimes wonders if God made the wrong call. If he somehow mixed my calling up with, say, Mary Kate Olsen or Joanna Gaines. Because we all know that celebrities have the easiest calling and feel no pain. (I am joking. Of course they feel pain. They just get to dress better and cry in bigger houses while in the midst of their suffering.) But we don't get to choose where God calls us, do we? What we do get to choose is how we respond. I dream of being the kind of woman who can respond joyfully. I want to be the kind of woman who says, "I am the handmaid of the Lord. May it be done to me according to your word." But instead I am the kind of woman who says, "Holy crap. Really?" I am working on that.

Something that helps me to stand strong on the frontline in this battle is to remember that God chose me for this call. Even if I think the calling sucks, even if I think I am not equipped for the role, even if I am afraid, he chose me because I am the best woman — the only woman — for the job. We have to believe that. We have to rise up to the call totally convicted, declaring whose we are and certain that his grace is enough to hold us up when all we want to do is curl up in a ball and wake up to it all gone. It also helps to recall the motley crew Jesus hung out with. The tax collectors, fishermen, prostitutes, sinners, lepers, murderers, betrayers, and thieves. A real neat bunch. My kind of crowd. I am sure they had never imagined in a million years what God had planned for them. I am sure they too felt wholly unqualified, much too weak, too small for the call. But even so, they responded. They responded quickly. So quickly that they left everything to follow him. Then I remember Mary. The teenage girl who had her entire life turned upside down and ended up changing the world because she didn't say "Holy crap, really?" when called, but simply "YES."

The struggle is real and the battle is fierce and the war continues to pull at me from both ends to this day. The thing about a game of tug-of-war? Someone has to fall. But it won't be me. If I am ever going to fall, trust me, it will not be into the depths of despair, but only into the loving arms of my Father, who I hear not only knows the definition of good, but works all things for it. With my Rosary in one hand and my latte in the other, I will march confidently into this battle knowing and believing that I have been created for this very moment. That God has wholly prepared me for such a time as this.

BATTLE PLAN

When you want to say, "Holy crap, really?" to God's calling, remember Mary. Hear her "yes." God's call to her to be the mother of his only begotten Son was not a mistake. He chose her. She had been set apart for such a time as this. Before she was perfectly conceived, sinless in her mother's womb, God was preparing her for this most awesome role. You are no different. Whatever it is he is calling you to, remember that you are the most perfect woman for the job, and he will supply you with every bit of grace you need to fight and win this battle.

WEAPON OF CHOICE

Rosary beads. I recently spoke with a Sister of Life. When I admired the long strand of Rosary beads that hung from her left side, she asked me if I knew why they wore them that way. "Warriors used to keep their best weapon — their sword — on their left side, and when they went into battle, they would reach to their left, and pull it out. The Rosary is our best weapon." And I agree. Keep your Rosary on you, in your car, sleep with it in your hands, and echo Mary's response: "I am the handmaid of the Lord. May it be done to me according to your word" (Lk 1:38).

Chapter 10

THE "IT'S NOT FAIR" BATTLE

"I consider that the sufferings of this present time are not worth comparing with the glory that is to be revealed to us."
— ROMANS 8:18

"It's not fair."

How many times a day do I hear that? Not from my children, but from myself! When I was younger, problems were unfair circumstances that got in the way of my getting what I wanted and deserved. The worst part of it all might not have been so much that I didn't get what I believed was owed to me, but that *someone else did*. That whole "weep when others weep" is so easy, but to "rejoice when others rejoice," when you are still weeping? So not fair, right?

When we are children and don't get our way, we stomp our feet, throw ourselves to the ground, scream at the top of our lungs. We might even shout in a burst of anger, "I hate you!" at the one who loves us most but refuses to give us the good things we want. Really good things, like the steak knife while we play hopscotch, or the lollipop while we run and play tag, or the plastic toy we are trying to pry out of our friend's hands. We extroverts always prefer to do this out in public, right? Preferably at a crowded mall or during Mass or in the grocery store checkout line. We may even drop like a sack of potatoes and go boneless right there in the middle of the parking lot, not caring about the moving cars or the people staring at us. I used to love it when my children would do that. It was not at all unsafe or embarrassing.

Thankfully, we grow up and out of these public tantrums and reactions to unfairness. But we still have them, don't we? Some like to rant on the internet, which always results in good, respectful, conversation, don't you think? Personally, I like to throw a more private tantrum, secretly, in my mind. I cry loud, and I let God know how utterly let down I am by his unfairness. I wonder what he could possibly be thinking when once again I am overlooked; when once again we are out of money; when once again I have a child in crisis; when once again I have to trim my beard. Because enough with the facial hair already, Lord, okay? I am a woman, and I should not have a beard. It isn't fair. It is just human nature, I suppose, how we want everything to be fair. Everything to be equal. No one preferred, no one with more, no one with better, no woman with a five o'clock shadow. Wouldn't life be so much easier if everything were fair? Wouldn't life be so much better if God were fair? Wouldn't I be so much more attractive if I didn't look like Moses?

I have a dear friend who many might believe has earned the right to say, "It's not fair." She is one of the most devoted and faithful to the Lord women I know. Unexpectedly and tragically, her sweet six-year-old daughter was taken from her arms and placed into the loving arms of Jesus. Thrown into this path of grief and suffering, she never missed a step, continuing to praise the holy name of Jesus, despite her painful circumstance. Her lot in life hardly seems fair. If she stopped going to church, or believing in God, or brushing her teeth, or simply breathing for that matter, the world would understand. However, she has chosen to respond to unspeakable unfairness differently. She not only continues to smile and believe in a good, loving Father, but she makes other people smile, and leads them to believe in the same good, loving Father. Not because she understands why God took her daughter, because she does not. Not because she is a better person than you or me. (Although she is better than me, actually, so scratch that last line.) My beautiful friend responds this way because she does not dwell on God's fairness, but rather she believes in his faithfulness. She holds onto the hope of God's promise, which was never that he was fair, but rather that he is just. She believed in his Word when life felt fair, and that same faith has not wavered based on circumstance. She stands on solid ground, and has since a young age, memorizing Scripture and drinking it in daily, because she is a faithful Protestant. Sorry, Catholics, but we really need to up our game when it comes to reading the Bible and memorizing God's Word. Catholics are capable of memorization too, you know. Also, for the record, I know she still brushes her teeth and is breathing because I sit next to her at Bible study, and she smells amazing and is very much alive. More so than most human beings I know.

We all have a choice as to how we respond to life's unfairness, and as I write, I am remembering not only the unfair situations in my life, but my misguided responses to each of them — reactions born out of my pride, jealousy, ego, and wavering faith. Too much thinking that I know what I need better than God does. Too much believing that my plan and timing is better than his. (Oh, Lord, don't get me started on your timing.) It's the whole *thy will* versus *my will*. This sinful pride directs how I choose to respond. This lack of faith has me choosing poorly. This jealousy eats away at my insides, turning my face away from God's, causing me to take a step out of the light and into the dark, closer to the evil one who has been scheming this response for me all along. Because he does that, you know. The evil one plants poisonous seeds in our hearts when we are not paying attention. He delights when we turn our backs against God. He is thrilled when we choose not to respond out of faith, trust, and humility, as our Blessed Mother does. He loves it when we focus on our neighbor who appears to be dealt a better hand of cards. He laughs as he watches us fall deep into the joyless pit of comparison while devouring an entire bag of multigrain tortilla chips and drinking the salsa straight out of the jar.

The struggle is real, folks. But praised be God, he is real, too! God is real, and when we stay awake to his presence, he is more powerful than any of the wickedness and snares of the devil. We have to remember that he is a God who keeps his promises, and that it's the devil's job to make sure we doubt his goodness in times of unfairness. This is all a part of the enemy's battle plan to rip us away from our Father, and good grief, but sure as the hair on my chin, I fall for it every time.

It is so crazy that I battle my own God, questioning his will for me, pointing out his mistake. It is crazy because deep down inside I know God's will is better than mine, and I know God does not make mistakes. Truth is, I am afraid. When God's plan doesn't match up with mine, I am reminded that I am not in control, and this scares me. One day while battling this out, I stumbled across a reflection by Bishop Robert Barron on a verse in the book of Jeremiah. You know the verse, even if you do not read the Bible. It is the one about the potter and clay. In Scripture, the potter is God, our Sovereign Maker. We are the clay, simple, humble, and apt to be shaped. The clay does not tell the potter what to do, but stays moist and workable, trusting in the hands of the One doing the shaping. Now, what really spoke to me was how he described the ingredients in the clay. He compared them to all of our life experiences, the painful, difficult, and unfair. He described these ingredients as necessary, as serving a divine purpose — to perfect us. Everything God wills and permits to happen in our life, every speck of the fair and unfair, is used to shape us into who we are meant to be.

You see, we can certainly battle this one out with God, and Lord knows, I have and do. When he shapes us into an unfair situation, we can fight against his hands, growing hard and prideful, making his work painful as he molds and forms us. Or we can believe in this Potter by remaining soft, humble, and accepting. We can allow him to do his work, despite not understanding why, trusting that he is forming us into a final creation way better than we can ever imagine. And this is so hard to do, isn't it? Putting aside ego and pride and knowing how my life should be is probably the greatest battle in my faith life, and the enemy of my soul knows it. The enemy is relentless in his attacks on me when unfair circumstances arise, telling me I deserve better, convincing me that God doesn't care, holding me face down in my bitterness and anger. When these attacks happen, if I do not quickly put on the armor of God and declare out loud that my Potter and Maker is shaping me into something awesome, I stand the chance of turning away from the incredible opportunity to be shaped into a heavenly sculpture for something lesser ... like a useless pinch pot, if even that. But most likely I am too hardened to be shaped into anything useful. Too dry to become what I was meant to be.

I don't know which place you are in right now. You may be the clay being easily molded, resting peacefully in the hands and the will of your Maker. Or maybe you are clay that has hardened, resisting the work of his hands, holding tight to your own will. Whichever you are, please know that I have been in both places. What I have discovered is that life is going to be unfair and painful regardless, so this battle really does come down to me and how I choose to respond. Am I going to walk blindly into battle believing the enemy's lies that a good Father should be fair and that my will is better? Am I going to turn my back on God when he doesn't immediately give me what I want, providing the enemy with a perfect target to take me down? Or will I march up to the frontline like a mighty warrior dressed for battle, standing on truth and the rock-solid belief that my Father is better than fair; he is just, and what feels like it's holding back on me is actually God doing his greatest work in me? The devil wants us to harden and to separate ourselves from our Father. He wants us to throw tantrums like children, to drop to the ground boneless and shout out, "I hate you!" to the One who gives us good things. He wants us to focus on the unfairness and remain in the dark. You have to remember this. Because fighting in the dark is never a good thing and dropping to the ground boneless will not win the battle.

We are not finished products by a long shot, sweet friend, but an incredible piece of art in the making. Life is never going to be fair, but that doesn't mean it can't be beautiful. Think about it. When all is said and done, and that glorious day arrives, and you are face to face with God, do you really want him to judge you based on fairness? Because good grief, I am screwed if he does. Especially if I am standing next to my teeth-brushing, Bible-quoting Protestant friend. Give me a just Father over a fair Father any day. A Father who, from the moment the slab of clay that I am hits the wheel, knows exactly what I need to become, and exactly who I am meant to be. It is so tempting to resist his hands when it hurts, but we have to press on — we must press on — and keep our eye on the end result. I don't know about you, but I don't want to go through this life as a slab of nothingness pointlessly spinning on a wheel, never taking the shape and form of what I am meant to be, all because I think life is not fair. I think it is fair to say that neither do you. So, let's get to know this just Father of ours, this awesome potter, more intimately. Let's resolve to quit fighting the "it's not fair" battle and be the soft clay that rests in his hands, trusts in his work, and looks forward to the masterpiece we are to become.

BATTLE PLAN

Is there something in your life right now that does not feel fair? Have you been striving to understand why God has put you in this hard place? Write it out, talk it out, bring it all to the Lord.

WEAPON OF CHOICE

The Shield of Faith. God knows what he is doing, and his plan for you is good. Protect yourself from thinking otherwise by praying with Proverbs 3:5–6: "Trust in the LORD with all your heart, and do not rely on your own insight. In all your ways acknowledge him, and he will make straight your paths."

Chapter 11

THE "WHERE THE HECK ARE YOU, GOD?" BATTLE

"Why do you stand afar off, O LORD?
Why do you hide yourself in times of trouble?"
— PSALM 10:1

I have a rock-solid faith ... until I don't. It is truly amazing (and by "amazing" I mean sort of embarrassing) how easily this faith of mine can be shaken. I want feet that stand firm on the ground. I want to weather the raging storm. At least, for the most part I do. For the most part I do stand firm, I do hold my ground. For the most part I do keep my eyes fixed on the Lord when the crashing waves sweep over me. But "for the most" part means "not always," right? It indicates that sometimes I don't. So in regards to the battle, "for the most part" means there is a chink in my armor. That means I am not fully protected. Marching to the frontline almost fully protected is just as dangerous as not being protected at all.

Would you rest your newborn in her car seat, then drive at full speed without ever strapping her in? Or only strapping her in sometimes? My guess is you would not. My guess is you would most likely over-protect her on a daily basis. So, if we fully protect the ones we love every day, why are we not fully protecting ourselves? Why do we march ourselves out onto the front line almost protected, and then act surprised when we find ourselves wounded?

A chink in one's armor refers to a specific area of vulnerability, a weakness somewhere in the suit. Keep in mind, a chink is not a chunk. It is not a large, obvious imperfection that you can see and immediately know you need to repair. A chink is super tiny, almost invisible to the eye. Half the time you have no idea it is even there. Like the leftover pork chops in the back of your fridge, or that extra tray of stuffing you put back in the oven to keep warm on Thanksgiving Day and kept it there until Christmas. So, you wake up and put on your armor feeling like you are Saint Joan of Arc or Wonder Woman and walk out the front door feeling like you've got this day. You are a warrior with a plan in your head and a $6 nonfat vanilla skinny latte with a double shot of espresso in your hand. Really, what could possibly go wrong?

Besides everything.

I absolutely walk around in this suit of armor. Shiny and strong and protected to the eye, but right where I am weakest, the teeniest and tiniest of hairline fractures hides. And it is not until I am blindsided by a trial, a tragedy, a trauma, any sort of unbearable suffering, that suddenly the invisible crack becomes visible. It is all I can see. It is all I can feel. Remember in chapter 10, when I talked about the way the enemy carefully plants the poisonous seeds? He does this because he knows your most vulnerable spaces, and that is precisely where he aims his flaming arrow. That weak spot, my friend, is the chink in your armor. It has a name. It has an emotion. It has a reaction most pleasing to the one taking aim. It is the very thing you struggle with the most, the very thing the enemy uses to pull you apart from Christ.

The chink in my armor is in my response. It is my immediate anger and doubt toward God in times of deep suffering. Specifically? The burden of suffering that is laid upon my children. I just don't understand it. I cannot comprehend in my own small, pea-brained human mind that wants everything to make perfect sense why an all loving God would ever place such burdens upon innocent children. Children, mind you, that I pray for unceasingly. I have prayed for them for years. I mean, I am not talking a quick little prayer here and there. I am talking hard core stuff, like novenas and consecrations and adoration and fasting from coffee (which, HELLO, that in and of itself should produce an immediate healing miracle and sign from above as far as I am concerned). I believe that a mother who prays is a serious weapon, so when these prayers appear to fall on deaf ears because Jesus left to use the bathroom or check his fantasy football lineup, I get a little ticked off at him. How on earth does he not hear me and fix things? How on earth does he appear gone when everything crumbles? How on earth is it that he not only permits painful things to happen, but that he wills them? It just doesn't add up, and it stirs up all kinds of anger and doubt that push grace out of reach.

The flaw in my armor goes deeper than anger or doubt, taking me into much more dangerous territory. When suffering does not make sense, when I feel like no one has any control at all, and when my confusion sends me reeling into a permanent state of code red, I do not believe that God is present. I am convinced that baby Jesus has left the house. I do not see him, or feel him, and I cannot even pray to him. Those solid feet are now sinking in the sand, and the crashing waves I thought I could manage now fill my mouth and nose until I can no longer breathe. It is there that I find myself utterly alone, sinking and drowning, and God is not there to reach out his hand and save me.

I hate this battle. This battle rattles every bit of me, as I try to hold on tight to what my heart knows is truth but my head is trying to make sense of. As my heart and head battle each other, an inner war breaks out. This is when I feel like I am that beautiful snow globe you might have had when you were a child — a fragile glass globe with the picture-perfect scene inside that completely disappears when shaken, becoming invisible to the eye. All you can see is the snow. All you see is the white. While you know that the beautiful scene is still there, you can only focus on the chaos of the blinding, white, absolute nothingness that fills the glass globe. Life can be like that snow globe. One hard, out-of-the-blue shake, and everything you knew to be real and good and perfect is gone. And it is terrifying, isn't it? This is what trauma does. This is what circumstances of extreme suffering and pain can do to us. They shake us up hard, out of the blue, causing such blinding confusion that the only thing that makes any sense at all is doubt in God's presence. Because, let's be honest, when life goes wrong, we need someone to blame. At least I do. While I might blame my husband for a lot of things, I can't blame him for everything. So I go to the One I love above all things, and I blame him. Because really, would a good Father allow such pain? Could a loving Father place such hideous burdens on his children? The only answer that makes any sense at all is either I have got it all wrong and he is not good, or even worse, it's all one big hoax and he is not real. Because if he were, he would be there. Better yet, if he were, he would not have allowed the pain in the first place.

My family has endured its share of trauma and pain, and I know that as life goes on, we will be called upon to endure even more. From illness, to financial burden, to senseless acts of violence and the repercussions of such incomprehensible loss, we will continue to battle. We will also continue to hold onto hope despite our circumstances. This is not easy. Each time I am shaken, the arrows fly directly at my weak spot, attempting to decrease my faith and pull me apart from the vine. I have often (even as I write) wondered, "Where are you God? I mean honestly. Where the heck did you go?" As I attempt to pray, and I read about his comfort and his presence in times of trial, you know what I do? I mock him. I laugh at him. I roll my eyes at Scripture. Then, like an obnoxious child, I turn my back on him and give him the silent treatment, because in that moment, I find zero comfort in any of his words. In fact, they frustrate me more because, first of all,

I don't want to be comforted in my pain. I want full pain removal! I also find myself choking on his promises because they leave me wondering if they are true for some, but not for all, and obviously, this sinner didn't make the cut. I find it nearly impossible to believe, when it feels like all hell has broken out under my roof, and I am literally dying on my filthy kitchen floor from the unspeakable pain, that *God is there.* Because, good grief, Lord, if you are there, how about you DO SOMETHING?

Up until yesterday, I believed the chink in my armor must be in my breastplate. It had to be somewhere close to my heart, because tucked into the deepest corners of my heart, where peace is found and the snow globe is still, I love Jesus. Before Jesus, I was self-focused, unfulfilled, searching for purpose in material things and other's opinions of me. I was the lost sheep wandering down the wide path, and he truly saved me. He pursued me relentlessly until he found me, and then he placed me on his shoulders and carried me back to the safety of my fold. He reminded me of my true worth. He restored my family. He redeemed me. He guided me toward the narrow path, and I cannot even begin to list the blessings that have been showered upon me since I chose to follow him. That is why I write about him. That is why I share my story. That is why I drive my children crazy to the point where they shout, "Why does everything have to be about Jesus?" — to which I answer, "Because everything is." He is my rescuer, my Good Shepherd, and I love him. So, clearly, it must be my heart that is under attack. It must be my heart that is being invaded when I turn on my Savior and believe he is not with me.

Yes, the heart must always be guarded. Lisa Brenninkmeyer's *Fearless and Free* Bible study opened my eyes to another perspective that I would be wise to take into serious consideration, should I care to win this battle. She quotes Dr. James Dobson, a licensed psychologist and a marriage, family, and child counselor, who says that pain and suffering are ultimately not what cause us the most damage. Rather, it is the confusion that arises in the trial. It is the confusion that "shreds our faith."

Finally, my confusion makes sense.

It is the snow globe. It is the shaking and the confusion that follow the trial that ultimately derail me. Because I can no longer see, and because nothing makes sense to me, the negative thoughts start to flood my brain, filling in the gaps that do not add up. Because I do not understand the story unfolding before me, I need to make up my own, one I can follow, one that I can understand. Psychologists call this "magical thinking," but this sort of distorted thought process only causes me to spiral into an abyss of despair and depression — and even worse, I can't even think about eating chips and salsa. In fact, I can't eat at all. It is that bad. So basically, if you see me and I am looking on the thin side, you can safely assume I am under attack. When under attack, I quickly forget about all the times that God was there for me. I immediately discount the numerous times he came to my rescue, not to mention those times he carried me to safety and I had no idea. I fail to recall that this God I claim "is not here" chose to be born as a baby and live among us and endure pain and suffering like us. I forget that the God I am so eager to follow when it leads to joy and happiness is also the God who asks me to follow him to the cross. When caught in battle with a chink in my armor, I forget that my good Father, with his own tear-stained face, is right there, weeping with me. He has not left me. In fact, he is right where the pain is.

Now is the time, sweet friend, to put on your helmet of salvation. Don't worry about messing up your hair, or whether or not you look good in hats. Just put the darn helmet on. In times of suffering and confusion we can't be vain. We need to discipline ourselves. We need to retrain the way we think by focusing on the positive, good, and undeniable ways that our God has shown up for us. We need to keep at the forefront of our minds our salvation, which was won for us by the very blood of Jesus Christ, who we believe has walked out on us. Trust me, I know this is hard to do, because I am the absolute worst at this. I remember to protect just about every part of me except my mind, which I leave open and exposed, an easy target. My mind is what gets the best of me. Ask my family, and they will tell you that their mother lives in a constant state of code red. It is just such an awful way to live, because it leads me right into enemy territory, far away from truth. Truth that we find in Hebrews 2:18, "Because he himself has suffered and been tempted, he is able to help those who are tempted." Or in Exodus 14:14, "The LORD will fight for you, and you have only to be still."

Ugh. Be still?

I don't like to be still because being still feels like nothing is happening. I am a doer. A mover and a shaker. I like to cross things off lists and get things done. Stillness doesn't feel productive. When my head is going crazy and I feel like my heart is being torn to shreds, and I am crying out to my God to save me from this hell I am living, call me crazy, but good grief, Lord, I need *something* to happen. I need some proof that I have not been forgotten and that the Words I have been reading and the prayers I have been whispering and the Gospel I have been preaching have not been in vain. I need to know that God is there with me, doing his thing, stepping into the gap, fixing every bit of my mess and brokenness. I do believe this is what so many of us battle. It is not so much that we think God has abandoned us, but rather we cannot believe that he isn't stepping in at exactly the moment we feel that he should. We don't want to endure the pain. We want him to remove it completely and quickly. And when he doesn't? Well then we just assume that he must not be there.

I had a particularly tough time in battle this week, and "particularly tough time" is putting it mildly. It was so tough that yesterday I woke up and refused to suit up. I didn't want to even look at my armor because I was so let down by my Father, so completely disappointed in the loser deck of cards he had dealt me, and I wanted him to know it. Not that I know how to play cards or anything, so really, you could hand me any combination of playing cards and I would have no idea if they were good or not, but you get the picture. Life was feeling beyond crappy and unfair, and I actually thought, "After all that I have done for you, Lord, *this* is how you treat me?" (Yes. I know. Take a moment of silence for me before continuing on. I am equally as horrified by my thoughts as you are.) But you know, this is what is so great about me, and by great I mean stupid and predictable. These ridiculous things that I blurt out to God in the privacy of my own distorted mind? They always wake me up just a little bit. They always catch me and shake me to my senses just enough that I can hear his voice responding, "What *you* do for for *me*? Hey sweet thing, have you even *looked* at the crucifix lately? Might want to put that latte down for a second and spend some time at the foot of the cross. Just sayin'."

Jesus and me? We talk back and forth like this a lot. It is a saving grace, actually. Because even if we are bantering in the sarcastic way that mimics conversations I have with my husband, we are communicating. By his grace alone, a channel between us has opened, and I am engaging in conversation with my Father. Even if I am doubting. Even if I am angry. Even if I am telling him of my plans to put his image on a milk carton and put out an Amber Alert because it has been made very clear to me that he is *gone* … I am talking to him. Now guess what? You don't talk to someone if you truly believe they are not there. You do not acknowledge what you do not believe truly exists. (This is when Jesus does the ol' mic drop in my face.)

I know that God is here … and there … and everywhere. When the unspeakable happens, when a hard truth is revealed, when you are out of chips and salsa, he is still there. You see, our God never promised we'd be free of trouble in this world, right? But he did promise that we need not be afraid because he would take care of the world. Our God never told us we would have to fight it out on our own, but to be still and he would do all of the heavy lifting himself. We are also reminded that whatever it is we are facing is going to feel like nothing in comparison to the weight of the glory that awaits us. Yet even with these truths, if you are anything like me, you still battle against it. You see, I want immediate relief. I do not like to hurt, I cannot bear to see my children in pain, and when in the midst of unbearable suffering, I do not want to know that I am being refined and he is at work and that all of this is going to turn me into some sort of incredible saint oozing with virtue. I don't want to ooze anything! I just want the freaking pain to go away. In fact, if I could go to sleep and wake up to a completely new set of circumstances (easy ones, with a side of guacamole and maybe longer legs), I would. I am working on this. I am working hard at remembering that God does not work the way I work, or think the way I think — and thankfully so, or we would all be in a whole lot of trouble.

The more I try to understand why he allows certain things to happen, the more I step into enemy territory, because, news flash: we will never understand the mind of God. Ever! This is when true faith is tested, where the rubber meets the road. Do I follow "party Jesus" who only turns water into wine, or multiplies the fishes and loaves, or is reclining at table having his feet washed with expensive oil? Or am I also willing to follow the "sorrowful Jesus," who was beaten and bruised, mocked and humiliated, who carried my sins on the cross, was crushed and killed, so that I could have eternal life? This, sweet friend, is the real battle. Is God there in the midst of your pain even when you do not see or feel him? Yes, he is. But are we willing to be still and trust that despite not feeling his presence, he is very much with us, and he has a good, even great, plan? Do we respond out of doubt and hold onto bitterness, or will we choose to respond out of grace and hold onto hope? The choice is ours. He remains the same, regardless.

Today, despite praying I'd wake up to a new set of circumstances, I woke to the same. But unlike yesterday, as soon as my feet hit the ground, grace swept in, and I reached for my armor. You can bet the first piece I put on was that stylin' helmet of salvation. You see, I cannot afford to lose this battle I'm in. Not when I am fighting for the people I love the most. Too much is at stake, so I will seal with truth every chink in my armor, staying awake to the fact that the enemy knows exactly where to aim and shoot, that he knows precisely how to pull me out of the protecting arms of my Father into the chaos and lies of this world. I need to stay disciplined in my thoughts and intentionally choose to follow Jesus more closely. Even if I do not see him, especially when I cannot feel him, I must choose to follow. In Philippians 1:29 Paul reminds us, "For it has been granted to you that for the sake of Christ you should not only believe in him but also suffer for his sake." So, when I choose to follow, it means I follow all of him — the joyful and the sorrowful. It means I follow him not only up the mountain, but also down into the dark valley. The comforting thing here that I need to hold onto is the knowledge that anywhere Jesus allows me to go, he has already gone. When suffering is where I am led, he has never been closer. He suffers by my side.

Have you ever wondered where God is? Are you wondering that now? If so, remember that snow globe. No matter how hard it is shaken, the scene is still there. No matter how hidden the landscape, it has not been removed. The shaking will not last forever. I know it feels that way, but remember, Jesus hung on the cross for three hours, and then he rose from the dead. He did not stay on the cross. He came down. Then he rose. Pain and suffering is meant to end. It will not last, I promise you that; and yes, I am writing that not only to convince you, but to convince myself. So, suit up with me, sweet friend. Put on your armor. Then be still. Do not move or fight, just simply stay in place. Close your eyes and ask him to comfort you so you feel it. Ask him for the grace to endure. Do not stop talking to him, even if you are angry and curse like a truck driver. He can take it. He's God. Do this, and in time, the chaos will subside. The confusion will give way. Faith will step in, and God's presence will be revealed.

Wait for the snow to settle. Then you will see. He was never gone. He was always there.

BATTLE PLAN

When my suffering does not make sense, I will be on guard not to allow the confusion that follows to shred my faith. I will work on disciplining my thoughts, refusing to focus on the pain and fear of the situation, but focusing on God and all of his promises.

WEAPON OF CHOICE

The Helmet of Salvation. I will reach for this, while meditating on Psalm 23:4. "Even though I walk through the valley of the shadow of death, I will fear no evil; for you are with me; your rod and your staff, they comfort me."

Chapter 12

THE BATTLE OF BOREDOM

"They who wait for the LORD shall renew their strength,
they shall mount up with wings like eagles,
they shall run and not be weary,
they shall walk and not faint."
— ISAIAH 40:31

When I was a kid, I was bored. All the time. I'm pretty sure I drove my parents crazy. On his more patient days, my father would assure me that this constant boredom was merely a sign of my extraordinary creativity and intelligence. On his not-so-patient days, he would throw me a pencil, point to a corner, and suggest I sit and stare at it. That pencil thing never went over so well. Fast forward almost forty years, and now I hear the cries of my own constantly bored children. I would hand them a pencil to a stare at, only being the unorganized mess that I am, I can never seem to find one — and handing them a bottle of wine to stare at just doesn't feel appropriate.

Ah, the battle of boredom.

Now let me clarify here. Boredom is not a sin. You are

not sinning if you are bored. What *can* be sinful are the not-so-great places and circumstances that boredom is capable of leading us to, and we need to stay awake to that. It is the attitudes and actions — like laziness and a sloth-like approach to life that are often born out of boredom — that are ultimately harmful. Sin, you know, doesn't always start out as a neon sign clearly marking the path to hell. In fact, the best, most effective schemes of the devil are the ones born out of sins that don't look so bad. That almost look *right*. This battle, which we are often dragging ourselves through completely unaware, is like an invisible poison, slowly leaking and spreading, filling our lungs, becoming the air that we breathe. It is a war that rages and aims to zap us of our passion and motivation, preventing us from getting up and doing God's will. We are reduced to slugs, really. The enemy delights in our apathy.

I am nearly fifty years old, and I often find myself still in this battle of boredom. But my eyes have been opened to a new boredom — one much more dangerous. The battle of *spiritual boredom*, which is far more troubling to my soul and cause for some serious armor. What does spiritual boredom look like? Well, it is not that I feel thrown deep into the depths of the valley, but it most certainly does not have me singing God's praises high on the mountaintop, either. This spiritual boredom leaves me out there floating somewhere in the middle. It is when I'm just sort of ... *there*.

Faith can be like this. One day it is a burning bush; the next day it is an empty well. Sometimes you can pinpoint exactly why: financial fears, worry over a child, marital troubles, health issues, loneliness, nine animals in your house that you regret ever bringing home. Other times you just aren't so sure. You just aren't feeling it. Maybe you have weathered a series of obstacles, and while you have survived the storms, for the most part you are feeling fatigued, and you are not overly sad or unreasonably depressed, you are just sort of ... *there*. No fire. Empty.

I hate this place. Even though I know and believe that Jesus can set a table in the desert, that Jesus can work with our dryness, that Jesus can cut through the heat and bring some cool breeze relief ... I hate it because it makes me feel like I am no longer connected to my faith. It makes me feel like I am not holding up my end of the spiritual deal. It makes me feel like I have fallen away, gotten out of practice, cut myself off from the vine. It is a joyless place. A place where you wake up, open your eyes, and rather than praise the Lord for another breath, another day with those you love, you sigh loudly and wish you had just ten more hours to sleep, because you have nothing of value to look forward to today, no reason to get up at all.

Do you ever feel like this?

Do you ever find yourself in this battle?

This place that I hate just might be the enemy's favorite place for me to be, and I believe it is safe to assume that I am not the only soldier down.

It will be worth your while to read the Gospel of Luke 8:19–21 right now. What sounds like Jesus dismissing his mother and disciples is actually his way of reminding us how very much we are loved by him: loved like he loves his own mother, his own brothers. (FYI: The disciples, like all of us, are Jesus' brothers and sisters. Mary did not give birth to them all, she only gave birth to Jesus. But Jesus loves them so much he considers them family. You know, like your bestie from high school who your kids call Aunt or Uncle. That kind of love. That kind of closeness.) In Bishop Barron's reflection on this Gospel story, he writes, "Friends, in today's Gospel Jesus identifies his disciples as his family." So let's just start there, shall we? Let's wake up and dress for battle by remembering this truth: you are (we are) deeply loved by Jesus. No matter where we wake up and find ourselves today. No matter what stinking, wretched mess we are buried beneath, no matter how broken and unfixable we believe we are, no matter how passionless and bored we feel to our core. We are loved, and we are to live loved. We are to live loved, as disciples of Jesus. (As a side note, I am currently reading *Uninvited*, by Lysa TerKeurst, who speaks of this idea of living loved. So I stole that from her. Because it is just so good.)

Perhaps we aren't living this way. Perhaps we aren't feeling the love and aren't following Jesus completely. I ask then — not just of you, but also of myself — *What or who are we following?* If we are not disciples of Jesus, whose disciples are we? Bishop Barron says, "Maybe it is money, material things, power, or the esteem of others. Perhaps it is your family, your kids, your wife, your husband. None of this is false, and none of these things are bad. But when you place any of them in the absolute center of gravity, things go awry."

Do you know what awry means? According to Webster's Dictionary, awry means "off the correct or expected course: amiss." You know what I think as I read this? I think the feeling of just being *there* ... the feeling of a dried-up well, an extinguished faith ... I think that happens when we allow things, people, worry, discouragement, to move into the center of gravity; to take the place where Jesus once was. It happens. We are human, and it happens. But, of course, Jesus is still there. If he were not, we wouldn't think twice about feeling disconnected or absent ... we would simply move on. But for whatever reason, he is no longer front and center in our everyday lives, where he belongs. When we wake up and think of ourselves, our kids, our problems, our jobs first, rather than of him, he has been replaced. This place — not deep in the valley, but not on the top of the mountain either — I think this is the place where things have the tremendous ability to go awry. The master of awry, the shadow behind the curtain who is orchestrating this plan to knock us off track and keep us from the course that God has placed before us, is the devil. Our seemingly harmless state of boredom has actually become a foothold for the enemy, and he smiles and laughs as he watches us. How he delights in our weariness, our lack of enthusiasm, and our quiet desperation. How he enjoys our idleness and distance from our God. All the while, we are completely oblivious to his scheme.

Putting Jesus before everything, especially our family, is no joke, no simple thing. It requires a grace upon grace that can only happen if we truly make the decision to follow Jesus and not the crowd. Luke tells us in his Gospel, "Then his mother and his brethren came to him, but they could not reach him because of the crowd." Oh, how I love those four words: *because of the crowd.* Because, oh man, are my head and heart ever so crowded. We all have a crowd, don't we? We all have people or circumstances or fears or even joys that get in our way, that stand blocking Jesus, that keep us from reaching him.

If you feel like I feel, if you realize this battle, here is a simple thing to do today: identify and call out your crowd. *What keeps me from making Jesus my top priority? What have I allowed to stand between my God and me? What is most important to me, if it is not Jesus?* These are good things to ask ourselves — as we stand in the middle of a war, not feeling it, spiritually dried up. Faith calls us to move. We cannot stand in one place forever. Not if we want to transform our lives, not if we hope to change ourselves and better the world. Not if we want to stick to the course that God has planned for us. *We need to move.* We need to go on mission.

Where do we go from here? Well, we have two choices: down into the deep valley, or up high on the mountain. Don't get me wrong. Both have their place. Both serve a purpose. Actually, my best prayers have been whispered in the blackest and deepest of holes, nose pressed down to the ground, body flat in the dust. There can be tremendous beauty and breakthrough when you become hyper aware of how incredibly broken you really are. The valley is often where I encounter his mercy. But if we are exhausted and depleted, and have given this boredom free range to lead us into harmful circumstances that disconnect us from our true life source, we miss his mercy, we fail to see this opportunity to grow stronger in faith. We can slump down to the ground and call it quits, making this darkness feel too painful, too impossible to cut through. But we always, always have a choice. Even in the darkness we can choose to *just be there* without Christ, or we can choose better: to *just be there* with Christ. The enemy wants you to sit in this slump, believing you are alone, that you have been defeated, that there is no choice, and that this is what your life will forever look like. But remember, sweet friend, the enemy is a liar. Jesus, our truth, however, is never more present and with you than when things feel darkest.

None of this is easy. I get it. Personally, I prefer the mountaintop feeling. Why can't God just plop us up there and keep us there? But if we are to be warriors for our God, followers of Christ, it means we suit up and courageously follow him everywhere. Jesus went to the top, and he went to the bottom. To get to either of these places, he had to journey somewhere through the middle as well.

I want to be a fierce warrior, and I want to be a follower of Christ. I want you to be, too. You see, I want us to win. I don't want us to just survive, I want us to be victorious. If we are going to win this battle of spiritual boredom, we must not give the enemy that foothold that he is way too eager to take. No matter how boring, passionless, or purposeless our lives might feel, we must keep Jesus front and center. We must push away the crowd and persevere in living loved, no matter where he leads us. Be it the beautiful banquet or the dry desert, we need to get up, suit up, and stay on course, trusting that our guide knows the best way. Believing that this middle ground that feels so dry and lifeless is a battlefield that God has entered in with us and for us. That he is right there fighting by our side, and that what we see as boring just might possibly be the grounds for some of his best work in us. I repeat, keep him front and center. Even if he has left you somewhere in the middle.

It is okay to feel like you are *just there* today. Just be there with Jesus. Because even in the desert, life still grows.

BATTLE PLAN

Jesus front and center, baby! Seriously. When you wake up, push away all of those other thoughts, to-do's, worries, negative thinking — all those things the enemy purposely plants to steer you off course. Call on Jesus. Think about him. Bring him into your day, no matter how boring it appears. Ask him to use this season of dry bones for good and then thank him for his protection, for keeping you on course.

WEAPON OF CHOICE

Let's reach for the main weapon in our arsenal, the Sword of Truth! This, sweet sister, is the Word of God. This is our fearsome weapon. When boredom leads us into harmful attitudes or situations, the sword of truth reminds us of what kind of life God calls us to lead and guides us away from a life gone awry. Meditate on Paul's words, as he addresses the Christian battle, because this battle is no joke — the (spiritual) struggle is real. "For though we live in the world, we are not carrying on a worldly war, for the weapons of our warfare are not worldly but have divine power to destroy strongholds. We destroy arguments and every proud obstacle to the knowledge of God, and take every thought captive to obey Christ" (2 Cor 10:3–5).

Chapter 13

THE "IT'S OKAY, GOD, I'VE GOT THIS" BATTLE

"Not that we are sufficient of ourselves to claim anything as coming from us; our sufficiency is from God, who has qualified us to be ministers of a new covenant, not in a written code but in the Spirit; for the written code kills, but the Spirit gives life."
— 2 CORINTHIANS 3:5–6

One of my favorite memories has to be the time my dear friend Krissy, mom of two toddlers, was pregnant with twins and on strict bed rest orders. *At Christmas time.* Now what you need to know about Krissy is that Krissy loved to plan. She spent her Saturdays out on the front porch with a cup of coffee, poring over recipes and magazines and planning out her entire menu and grocery list for the week. She loved to throw big parties, cook delicious dinners, and decorate her home. With a keen eye for detail and a love for making all things fun and beautiful, she really was like a brunette Martha Stewart, minus the jail time. So you can imagine how being still, just weeks before Christmas, absolutely killed her. There was so much to do, and only she could do it. Only this time, she couldn't. She had to depend on others.

One afternoon, Krissy called me in tears. She had sent her husband out to purchase the Christmas wrapping paper. "FOIL PAPER?" she cried into the phone. "Laura, he bought FOIL wrapping paper! I can't wrap my gifts in this crap!" She continued to cry and repeat over and over again, "FOIL? FOIL? How?" She was like Joan Crawford in *Mommie Dearest*, completely undone by the wire hangers. I contemplated driving to Krissy's house in that moment, fearful she might wrap her own head in the foil and throw herself the oven.

Krissy wrapped her gifts in foil that Christmas, and even so, hard to believe, the baby Jesus was born. Foil and all.

We all like to do the things we enjoy doing the way that we like, and that is fine. We all like to feel like "we've got this" and are in control, and that is okay, too … some of the time. Where the danger lies is in how deep the roots of our self-reliance go. Because like Krissy, we are not always going to be able to rely on ourselves. At one point or another, we will have to depend on others. Kind of like the summer my flight from a Florida business trip didn't make it back home in time for me to pack up my two kids for their first ever sleepaway camp experience in the Berkshire mountains. This incredibly daunting task was now completely left on the shoulders of my poor husband. Turns out, the kids had a great time, despite the fact that they spent a week of cold nights on a hard cot with no blankets, and days running and swimming at the lake and pool with wet feet sockless in sneakers because they had no flip-flops. They came home freezing and limping from some sort of unidentified foot fungus, but even so, they managed to suck it up and have the time of their lives. Now, if I had been home in time, they would have had extra blankets packed, and flip-flops in five different styles and colors. But I was not back in time, so instead of sleepaway camp, my kids basically played the game of *Survivor*, and needless to say, neither one of them found the immunity idol. The point here is not that my husband failed, but that at one point or another, we all have to turn over that self-reliance badge we proudly wear, and pin it on someone else. Every once in a while, we will be asked to let go of the trust we have only in ourselves and dole it out to another. Even if it means we wrap our gifts in that awful foil paper. Even if it means we send our precious children off to camp like we are Jeff Probst announcing, "Survivors ready?"

Maybe you are thinking, "This hardly sounds like a battle, Laura." After all, self-reliance is a good thing. We *should* self-rely. We *should* be strong and capable. We *should not* depend on others — even the Catholic Church will tell you not to put your hope in people or things, because people and things will always disappoint. But then here is the question I have for you. If we are not to put our hope in other people, then who are we to place our hope in? Ourselves? We are people too, right? Good grief, let me just put this out there: you my friend do not want ever to put your hope in me. Just ask my dog, Copper. Every time I let the poor pup out to pee, I completely forget. It is so weird, and other than old age and losing my mind, I have no idea how every time I let him out I walk away and forget about him. Cut to hours later, when I'm irritated by "the neighbor's obvious neglect of their dog," and I find myself asking the kids, "Whose stinking dog is barking outside like that? So rude!" So again, don't put hope in people. But then what should we put our hope in? Our jobs, achievements, talents, or bowls of chips and salsa? A big "no" to that as well, because those are just things. Yes, even the chips and salsa, though I agree, it is so hard to believe because they are just so good and make life so much better.

The Bible tells us we are to put our hope in Jesus. As we read in Hebrews 6:19, "We have this as a sure and steadfast anchor of the soul, a hope that enters into the inner shrine behind the curtain." So there needs to be the point where we look at our lives and the things that we do and hold onto so tightly and ask ourselves, "Is this something I can let go of?" The battle, my friend, known or not, is between our self-reliance and our God-reliance, our self-confidence, and our confidence in God. If you were to take a step back and have a good look, would you find that you are able to rest in God's work, or are you only satisfied when you are able to rest in your own work? Are we relying on God at all?

I think for most of us, this battle starts at a very young age. We all want to be the hero, right? We all want to be the leading role (or at least I do). We all want to be the juicy patty in the cheeseburger. We all want to do things on our own and prove to the world that we can, and of course we all want to be praised for how good we are at getting it all done, all by our own strength and talent. Because, really, who wants to be stuck in the last riser of the chorus in the big show of life? Not me! Who wants to be the wilting lettuce in the big juicy cheeseburger of life? No way, Jose! Who wants to let other people do things and get the praise and glory for it while we stand off on the sidelines unrecognized, when the truth is we could do it so much better? I'd rather die a death by foil wrapped around my head than not be noticed! It is a natural thing, I think, to feel this way. (Maybe not the dying by foil part, but you know, I was being dramatic to make a point.) I have to admit that even as I write I can hear it — can you? *Pride.* You see, relying on yourself fully and completely, while seeking all the praise and glory, as the world encourages us to do, is actually a big-time spiritual battle. When self-reliance runs the risk of becoming our primary source of self-esteem, or when it becomes the only thing that gives us our worth and sense of purpose, we eliminate God from the picture and replace him with our own striving. This battle of self-reliance is worse than it might appear, my friend, because it leads us to pride. Pride, no matter how big, fabulous, and colorful the parades for it might be, is actually not a good thing. It's actually one of the seven deadly sins.

Here I'm going to do something that I really never do, which is back up anything I have to say with actual Church facts or definitions. I'm more of a train-of-thought kind of girl, a "dump out my heart" type of rambling writer, not the intelligent, intellectual, studious kind, who actually knows what she is talking about. However, I think it is important before marching further into this battle, that we understand what pride, according to the Catholic Church, means. The *Catechism of the Catholic Church* defines pride as "an inordinate self-esteem or self-love, which seeks attention and honor and sets oneself in competition with God" (CCC 1866).

When your child goes down the slide for the first time, and you jump up and down clapping your hands, shouting out, "I am so proud of you!" that is not a sin. An overreaction, maybe, because I mean really, a grapefruit can go down a slide. But hey, I get it. I did it, too. We all do. Because we love our kids, and we are proud. But you see, the pride you feel when your kid goes down the slide is not about your own self-love, or about you at all, but about praising another outside of yourself, born out of love. You are acknowledging an achievement that is not of your own doing. But when you take full credit for anything good in you — be it your achievements, talents, whatever — without ever turning to God and saying, "Thank you" … well, then we have a problem. We read in 1 Corinthians 4:7, "For who sees anything different in you? What have you that you did not receive? If then you received it, why do you boast as if it were not a gift?" And in 2 Corinthians 3:5, "Not that we are sufficient of ourselves to claim anything as coming from us; our sufficiency is from God." Relying on ourselves or even being proud are not completely bad things. But when we take full credit for what we have done, without ever showing gratitude to God who made it all possible in the first place — that's when things go wrong. It is when we boast of our talents as if they come from us, without acknowledging the Giver of the gift, and that we received it freely — that is when we are spiritually under attack. When self-reliance bleeds into pridefulness, we have once again entered into enemy territory. You are going to need to be suited up in way more than a rainbow tutu and flag to protect yourself.

So, what to put on? Well, I think we need to backtrack a little bit here and be sure of what we already know and what pieces of armor we are already wearing. We know we are in a daily battle, right? I hope so. If not, this will be my first and last book. We know that the enemy loves to attack us with lies: lies about our worth, lies about our identity, lies about God our Father and how he is good and for us. So, if the flaming arrows of lies are flying at us constantly, hopefully we have already put on that belt of truth and are keeping it on! Do what I do, and just sleep in that darn belt. Seriously. Keep it on at all times. Because the enemy of our souls is not working hard and spinning all these plates because he wants us to hate God. He's much more subtle and cunning than that. With his enticing whispers and the way he makes wrong look right, his desire is for us to be so confused by what truth even is that we fall into the trap of having to trust ourselves more than we trust in God. So please, before you step into the battle of self-reliance, tighten up that belt around your beautiful waist. If you don't feel like you have a beautiful waist, that's the devil talking, and all the more reason why you should be wearing the belt. Your waist is beautiful because you are beautiful — and God made all of you. Own it and believe it and tighten that belt. You look good in it.

Now we reach for the breastplate of righteousness. Don't worry about the size of your breasts, this plate is a one-size-fits-all. All pieces of our armor are important, but the breastplate might be my favorite, mainly because it is so slimming — but also because the world today is tough on us when it comes to things like truth and righteousness. Truth has become relative, and God's righteousness has been replaced with self-righteousness. So what happens is I begin to think that it is my own righteousness, my own deeds and good acts, that make me worthy. Worthy to simply exist on this planet, but even more so, worthy enough to earn God's approval and love. That's why I resist help from others. I have something to prove and earn. What a booby trap! Sweet friend, there is nothing that you or I could ever do to earn our way into heaven. Trying to impress God by my good acts and righteous deeds is an embarrassing waste of time, not to mention completely against everything I claim to believe. If I were to even attempt to stand in front of

God to present him with all those great things I proudly did all by my own strength, well ... I would not be able to stand. Why?

Open up your Bible to Isaiah 64:6 and read this with me: "We have all become like one who is unclean, and all our righteous deeds are like a polluted garment. We all fade like a leaf, and our iniquities, like the wind, take us away." When we stand before God on that glorious day, he is not going to be looking at our list of self-attained accomplishments. Our deeds do not compare to God's deeds! They are filthy rags. What he will be looking for, however, is the measure of our faith. He is going to ask, "Do you believe in me? Do you believe in my Son? Do you know that by grace you have been saved and that every good gift you received on earth came from me? Did you point others to you or did you point them to me? Did you trust in yourself or did you trust in me? And did you ever say thank you?"

The truth is, we are already righteous by our faith in Jesus Christ. But when the world does all that it can (and it is doing it all too well, might I add) to remove God from everything, this battle grows bigger and bigger. Yet it is a silent battle, because it is acceptable. Self-focus has become a good thing. In 2013, the word of the year was "selfie." Today, we are greatly encouraged to be intentional about self-care. None of these things, in their own right, are bad. I've gotta say that, personally, I am not a fan of the selfie. Mainly because my teeth look like a scarecrow's (Do scarecrows have teeth?) and there is no stick long enough to get a good angle of my face that doesn't highlight my beard. But it's not just that. It's what we do with our selfies that bothers me. We post them. Lots of them. We put the focus on self. Then we wait for the comments. Let me say this, dear sister. You do not need the approval of anyone when it comes to your face. It drives me crazy when I see my daughters (and I have sons, but let's be honest, the boys are not taking nearly as many selfies as the girls) posing and making that duck face and constantly focusing the lens on themselves. I keep telling them that when they have the urge to take a picture of themselves they should take one of Jesus instead. (They love that idea and don't roll their eyes at me at all.) As for self-care, well, yes, we do need to be mindful of that for sure. But I find that most self-care out there is directed at the body and mind, not enough of the soul. A whole lot of "what you can do to better yourself" with zero mention of God's major role in it all.

Slowly and silently, this push toward self — self-reliance, self-righteousness — is encouraging us to depend only on ourselves for feeling good, and for becoming strong, confident women. We are being sold the lie that we can do it all on our own, it is all up to us, and we do not need anybody else to help us. Ultimately, we are being asked to lose all trust and confidence in God and place it all in ourselves. If this isn't a surefire way to lose the battle, I don't know what is. Look, I want nothing more than to be a confident and strong woman. I want nothing more than that for my own daughters. But never at the expense of cutting the branch off the vine and leaving God out of the picture. Not at the expense of believing I am in competition with God. Because it doesn't work. My worth and self-esteem are not based on my accomplishments. My ticket to heaven and eternal happiness is not based on how I white-knuckled through it all with no help whatsoever.

In fact, the more I ask for help, the more grace I am given. The more I allow others to step in and serve, the stronger we all become. Do you know that every time you hold tight to something because you think you can do it best, you deny another sister in Christ the opportunity to serve the Lord? Let's not be so self-reliant that we become hoarders of grace. Let's not be so focused on self-creation that we leave out the Creator.

If I had to guess, without knowing you at all, I would say you are in this silent battle right now. I think we all are. We are women. We love to have control. We thrive on hearing, "I don't know how you do it all," because in our distorted images and identity, it feeds our self-esteem. We wear this badge of accomplishment like it is a reflection of our worth, as if this self-reliance of ours is actually something good. But it isn't. You know what is good? Jesus. Jesus is good. He is our help. Psalm 121:2 clearly reminds us of this: "My help comes from the LORD, who made heaven and earth." If we did not need his help, than I am guessing he wouldn't have bothered with the Incarnation, Passion, or Resurrection. But he did.

There is nothing in this world that that will ever be good if it cuts us off from Jesus. There is no battle we will ever win if we do not abide in Christ. Open your Bible to John 15:5 and read it and memorize it and tattoo it on your breastplate: "I am the vine, you are the branches. He who abides in me, and I in him, he it is that bears much fruit, for apart from me you can do nothing." You hear that? Nothing. Now I know what you are thinking. You are thinking, "That is so not true! I rely on myself completely, and I always get things done, and I DO accomplish many things!" I am sure that is true. But Jesus is not talking about doing things that matter on earth. He is talking about things that hold eternal value. Things that truly matter in the end. We must always abide in Christ if our goal is to be eternally victorious. We must be open to the help he offers, the help that can only come from him. He is here right now to help us, constantly putting angels and saints and all kinds of everyday people in our path, to serve as his hands and feet, for us to rely on. Accepting help, or handing over a project or task (even when we know we could do it better) is not a weakness. In fact, it the greatest act of love and surest sign of your trust in God. As sisters in Christ, we are commanded to build up the kingdom of God here on earth, not the kingdom of self.

So, strap on that belt of truth and squeeze into your breastplate, sweet friend. Every time someone tells you, "Wow, I don't know how you do it all on your own," let them know that you don't. Point them in the direction of grace. Show them the face of the One who makes all good things happen. Then go ahead and post a selfie of you with Jesus. Your kids will love it.

BATTLE PLAN

I will look deeper into myself, examining those things I hold too tightly. I will ask if the reason I hold onto them is to build up God's kingdom, or to feed my self-worth. I will see everyone who offers me help as sent by Jesus, and I will allow them the opportunity to serve.

WEAPON OF CHOICE

The Breastplate of Righteousness. Wear this beauty with your belt of truth, and stand confident and strong in his righteousness as you meditate on 2 Corinthians 3:5. "Not that we are sufficient of ourselves to claim anything as coming from us; our sufficiency is from God."

Chapter 14

THE BATTLE OF TRUSTING IN HIS PLAN

*"Trust in the LORD with all your heart,
and do not rely on your own insight.
In all your ways acknowledge him,
and he will make straight your paths."*

— PROVERBS 3:5–6

I almost gave up on prayer. Not because I stopped believing in its power, but because God had finally made it all very clear to me. He was not, in any way, shape, or form, going to answer the prayer in the way I had specifically instructed him to. I didn't give him my plan just once, but often. Daily. For years. Through hard and soft tears. The same prayer, the same instructions, written out so clear and concise a flipping monkey could follow them. Despite all of my efforts, God still has not answered my prayer. He has failed to follow through with my plan.

I know that God is divine. In his divinity he hears, and he answers in the best, most perfect and tailored way possible for me. At least, that is what I continue to tell myself. Because it can't be just me, can it? Please tell me that I am not the only follower of Christ who stops every five feet and yells, "You missed a turn, Jesus! I think we should have turned back there! That road looks a lot safer, don't you think?" Anyone else out there question the road he has laid out for you? Anyone else ever feel like Jesus' way takes you through that one unsafe neighborhood your mother warned you about? That dark street you go out of your way to avoid? That must be the "man" part of our Savior — unable to follow a woman's directions.

I have found myself in what feels like an endless season of questioning God more than trusting God. Of giving him my commands in place of following his. I have been on this battlefield for quite a while, and if I am being honest, I gotta say, I have been poorly deflecting the enemy's arrows. In fact, I have been removing my armor each time I feel that doubt creep in. I remove my armor one piece at a time, deliberately undressing myself like a defiant child, all out of my anger and disappointment in a God who claims he hears and answers my prayers but never seems to come through. These arrows that pierce are some of the most soul-wounding because they aim to convince me that my God is not listening. That prayer does not work. That I am a fool to have been bowed down on bended knees for so long asking for the impossible. That God has better and bigger battles, other people to protect and fight, that my problems are insignificant. That this story of mine has a tragic and terrifying ending no matter how hard I pray for it not to.

It is amazing how we can so easily put our trust in things other than God. I listen to that GPS voice in my minivan and go exactly where she tells me to go, even though she is not a real person and even though I have absolutely no idea where I am. (For the record, I never know where I am. I have zero skills when it comes to directions, and I guarantee you that if the correct way to go is right, I will go left. It is amazing that I can find my own front door, really.) So, I fully rely on the generated woman's voice in my car to get me where I am supposed to be, safely. Yet I pull away from God and shut down prayer precisely when I find that, despite the praying, I am not feeling safe.

Here lies my problem. Right here is where I recognize I am standing on the frontline naked with a hardened heart, shouting out commands with zero intention of listening to where he tells me to run for protection. Because Jesus' way never feels safe. His way takes me on turns and hills, and when he whispers, "Be not afraid," I want to shout out, "Then, dude, take me another way!"

When I am being truthful — when I can sit completely still in front of Jesus, pretending to be nothing other than the hot mess that I am — I can tell him this. I can tell him, "Your way frightens me — and by frightens, I mean scares the s★★★ out of me. Your way is too hard. Your way doesn't feel good to me. Why do you continue to put me in these scary situations when I have been praying for comfort and safety? For healing and wholeness? Things I *know* you are capable of because, by the way, I read your book. All those lepers and the blind you clean up and fix, not to mention the dead people you raise? The freaking *dead*! Good grief, what is it about my specific prayer that you just can't seem to answer? You are not a good Father to do this to me. You can't possibly be. Screw prayer. It doesn't work, anyway."

It is always when I do this, when I have this hissy fit and toddler tantrum, that God does what every smart gentleman knows to do. He stays quiet. He lets me vent. He does not storm out of the room insulted by my lack of faith and my four-letter words. He does not try to fix me, because let's be honest, in these moments we are not really looking for solutions, only opportunities to be pissed off and make sure everyone knows it. Then, when I am finished, he brings someone to my mind that this sad sack of a crying mess desperately needs. He reminds me of his mother. Of gentle Mary. Off in the distance, at the foot of the cross, I see her. Standing. The same road that began with an angel and her "yes" led her to stand at the foot of the cross — the cross her son was nailed to. The nails that were my sins pierced through his hands and feet. That path was not easy. That path did not feel good. That path had no Starbucks for a quick energy boost. That path certainly was not safe.

Yet, she followed his plan.

He rose. What was under her heel? The crushed head of the enemy.

There was no hissy fit or tantrum. She never tried to convince God to take her another way. Her prayer was nothing other than her *fiat*, her "yes," her desire to do his will.

Even while writing this, in the back of my mind I hear the evil one telling me, "Yeah, but sweet thing? You ain't no Mary. You can't possibly respond like her. Go back to your chips and salsa worship and forget the useless prayer." All too often, I believe him. All too often, I go through prayers like I am reading my grocery list. I say them, but don't pray them. Do you ever do this? If so, I totally get it. This prayer thing? Weird, right? Because really, what is the point in praying for years if the prayer is never answered? How stupid are we? But the thing is, if we believe in God the Father, Christ the Son, and that he was conceived by the Holy Spirit, born of the Virgin Mary, suffered and died and then rose again so that we could have eternal life, well … then calling it quits on him and prayer is not as cut-and-dried as it appears.

Turning my back on him — no matter how angry I am — for prayers unanswered isn't as easy as it sounds. Why? Well, because I know his story — and because I have intentionally sought him out, I have actually come to grow quite fond of him. We are friends. He is my Father. Even though he doesn't always give me what I want, I still love him. Relationships are work, so if we fail to keep our eyes on the entire big picture here, we easily get tripped up on the present obstacle. We have to remember this, sweet friend, don't we? We have to remember the end of this love story. By we, I mean me, because right now, I have nearly forgotten. Right now, all I can see is a dark and rocky road that appears to have no end, that appears to lead to pain, that feels like the least safe road I have ever taken in my whole entire life. That is why God's reminding me of Mary is brilliant. Life-saving, really. Because when I place myself with Mary, when I remember that this story is one of love, that the only motive for every small bit of the cross was and will always be love, I can loosen my grip on the doubt the enemy is feeding me and tighten my grip on the hope the cross offers. I can focus on just one more small step, rather than the overwhelming length of road ahead. I can remember that even unsafe stories have beautiful endings. That prayers in his will are never left unanswered.

Love does this, wouldn't you agree? Love takes us to hard places. Love leads us down paths that feel wrong. Love demands that we lose our instructions, throw away our plans, and follow the GPS implanted in our hearts, knit into our deepest selves. Sometimes, love means doing the exact opposite of what our feelings and emotions beg us to do.

Do you find yourself in this battle? Because I swear, this is a fight I find myself in daily. This is a war that requires mucho endurance. I am sorry, but it just goes against everything in me to allow unpleasant things to happen and to accept them with grace. To respond to another unanswered prayer gratefully, assured that my Father knows best. To face suffering head on and say, "Hello suffering! Happy you are here! I know you are going to serve some incredible purpose!" But even at my snarkiest, I feel that tug — that gentle reminder — that pull to my heavenly mother. Think about it. You hear no stories of Mary screaming out, "Take my son down from that cross!" You hear no stories of Mary grasping at his feet, pulling him from the wood, trying to stop it all from happening, screaming, "He is innocent, you idiots!!! This is all so incredibly unfair and wrong!" All we hear is her "yes" to God's plan for her — and for her Son. All we hear is that she says, "Do whatever he says." All we hear are her footsteps as she accompanies her son on his walk to be crucified.

Then, she stands. Her standing is so brave, so powerful, so drenched in trust … you can hear that, too.

We are all such good planners, aren't we? We are all really good at giving orders, handing out instructions, and finding the easiest way to our destination. But when we rely

on ourselves to get where we need to be safely, we shut out
the One who has already mapped out our route and written
our story. We ignore the voice of the One who walks ahead,
behind, and all around us. We turn away from the One who
promises he knows the plans, and that his plans are "for welfare
and not for evil, to give you a future and a hope" (Jer 29:11).
I know. Sometimes our trials demand a trust of us that seems
superhuman. Downright impossible. Our knee jerk reaction,
encouraged by the one who throws the arrows, is to pull back,
to stop praying, to give up. But sweet friends, this is when we
are called to persevere and endure. This place right here? We
can make it enemy territory and march in place, leaving our
weapons next to our night stand, or we can make it sacred
ground and solid foundation, marching forward dressed for
battle trusting we are not in this fight alone. We can listen to
the orders of the one who would love nothing more than for
us to believe prayer is useless and that our route is better than
God's, or we can lean in closer to our good Father — who
knows we are frightened and who promises to protect us —
and continue to let him lead. Let us not settle for a cheap tour
guide or incorrect map when the raging war heats up. This
is the point in the battle when we need to stand strong with
Mary, rooted in the Gospel, fully armed.

These, my dear sister, are the roads we need to drive down,
trusting not on our own understanding, but pressing into the
sacred heart of the One whose understanding is higher than
we can ever reach or comprehend. We need to trust God more
than we trust our own safe plans, so that when all is said and
done, it will be his voice that says, "You have reached your
final destination." We will be safe, we will be sound, and we
will be standing.

BATTLE PLAN

Remember Mary. Walk this unsafe path with her. When you do not trust God's plan for you, and you feel afraid, and all you want to do is throw prayer out the window, tell Mary. She will bring your prayers to her Son for you. She will stand with you at the foot of the cross.

WEAPON OF CHOICE

Time to put on your shoes! Not your cute strappy sandals, because they will not protect. Definitely not your flip-flops, because they are not actual shoes. (Really, why are we wearing them to church, airports, and restaurants? Save them for the pool.) I am talking about your "gospel shoes." The Sandals of Peace. The shoes we wear so that we can confidently walk the same path that Jesus walked, recalling that the ending is good. The shoes that we put on trusting that our Lord's path is the surest way, the only way that will lead us to exactly where we belong.

Today, meditate on these two verses: "He who trusts in his own mind is a fool; but he who walks in wisdom will be delivered" (Prov 28:26); and "He who says he abides in him ought to walk in the same way in which he walked" (1 Jn 2:6).

Chapter 15

THE "CAN I STILL BE ME IF I'M TRYING TO BE HOLY?" BATTLE

"If anyone is in Christ, he is a new creation; the old has passed away, behold, the new has come."
— 2 CORINTHIANS 5:17

Are holy people creepy? Absolutely! Well, some of them. But not all of them. As Catholic speaker Chris Stefanick says in regard to the creepy holy: "They were creepy *before* they were holy." What can I say? Creepy people exist. There are creepy teachers. Creepy doctors. Creepy celebrities. Creepy boyfriends. Creepy mothers. Creepy neighbors. Creepy is everywhere. So, of course, as long as the Catholic Church is universal and welcomes everyone inside her doors, there will be creepy in the Church. But creepy does not equal holy. It's not like being creepy is a prerequisite to leading a holy life.

But we do this, don't we? We stereotype, and we assume that a person who strives to be holy must be a little bit off, because, honestly, for the most part people have no idea what holiness even means.

That was made very clear to me one lazy summer afternoon, poolside with a girlfriend. We were on our second pitcher of sangria (don't judge), laughing and joking and having a grand old time, when it came up in conversation that I attended daily Mass.

"As in … every day?" she asked.

"Yup, 9:00 a.m.," I said as I poured myself another glass of sangria.

Well, from that moment on, anytime this friend introduced me to a new person, she got all stupid animated, would lean in, and as if she had the breaking news on the Matt Lauer story, would blurt out, "Laura goes to Mass every day! Can you believe it?" Sure, this might sound nice that she acknowledged my faith — but it was not. It was not nice at all. It was more of a "can you believe that someone like *her* is religious?" Because I know this might be hard to believe, but I am a pretty outgoing person. I love to talk, I love to have fun, and I love sangria by the pitcher. I love to laugh, and I love even more to make other people laugh. I suppose in her mind, I did not fit the "religious woman" mold, mainly because … I was joyful. Yes, I will admit that back in the day, my joyful humor might have crossed a few lines. Okay, not "might have crossed," absolutely crossed. Jumped right over. All of the lines. I crossed them all. So, looking back on this season of my life, I can understand how my social behavior seemed contradictory to the behavior of a Christ follower. But despite how uncomfortable and awful this woman made me feel, I will go ahead and humbly throw her a bone. Only by the grace of God, by the way, am I able to do this — to throw that bone without purposely aiming for the back of her head. Because humility is *so* not my spiritual gift. Hanging on to bitterness and resentment is. Just ask me to tell you the story about the woman who called me "rowdy" five years ago on a field trip. You'll see how gifted I am at hanging on.

Even as I began to clean up my act and acknowledge that

lines were actually meant to serve as boundaries, not hurdles to leap over, people continued (and continue) to remain shocked that "someone like me" would be striving for holiness. What exactly is someone like me? Well, like I said, someone who likes to have fun. Someone who truly enjoys a good sense of humor. Someone who has a current haircut and knows that scrunchies are no longer meant to be worn outside of the house, or ever at all. Someone who does not homeschool because I can't do fourth grade math, and if I were home all day with four kids I cannot promise we would all survive. Someone who enjoys a cheap glass of wine and a margarita on the rocks with a little bit of salt. Someone who goes to TJ Maxx more than she should. Someone who likes to dance at the grocery store. Someone who can't help but use a certain four-letter word because there are those times in life when "good grief" or "sugar fudge" will simply not suffice. So basically? Someone like me is most likely not too unlike someone like you, and most everyone else. Except for that sweet Protestant friend I talked about in chapter 11. She's in a class of her own because she actually does say "sugar fudge" and is good at reminding me that that my words ought to be pleasing to the Lord, and well, all I can say to that is, "Sugar fudge, the woman is right." Bless her heart.

As I grow in my faith I absolutely feel the weight of this battle. Can I be holy, and still be me? Can I be a follower of Christ without people thinking I am creepy? Does dying to self mean no more margaritas? Does being religious mean I have to be humorless? Before I give you my answer to that, I think it is important that we understand what holy is and, even more so, what holy is not. According to the Bible Dictionary in the back of my Saint Joseph Edition of *The New American Bible* (that I received as a wedding gift twenty-one years ago, and *just* today discovered — not the Bible, but the dictionary) "the term 'holy' is applied to anything that is consecrated to God." (Makes you think twice about exclaiming "holy s%$!," doesn't it?) The very basic meaning of holy is "set apart" or "dedicated to God." Nowhere in my Bible's definition does it describe holy as being perfect, void of fun, and fashion-challenged. Nor does it include a vow to lead a boring life. I think the word holy has a negative side to it, implying that a holy person thinks they are better than others. I would also bet that most people consider holy ones as unapproachable or uncreative — the kind of girl a guy wants his mom to meet, but not the kind of girl he wants to take to the prom. Here is the deal. We can belong to God and still have fun. We can be "set apart" and still be an awesome prom date.

It is important to point out that holiness is not just about our moral behavior — our overspending, our cheating and stealing, our drinking and dancing, our sexual proclivities, our pro this or pro that. Please do me a favor, and do not replace the Word of God with the script from *Footloose*. Do not listen to the lie of the world that convinces us that a holy life is impossible and the Catholic Church's teachings are outdated and hateful. Because that lie? It is a huge part of this battle. The enemy delights in that false definition. The enemy wants us to turn our back on holiness and not even consider striving for it. Why? Because holiness, in the simplest terms, is about our relationship with God. The focus was never meant to be on what we are prohibited from doing, but rather, on the awesomeness we are called to be and do. When we abide in Christ, we can be and do anything. Nothing is impossible for God. Christ lives inside of each and every one of us. The best news of all? We belong to him! Sweet, holy sister of mine, do you even comprehend that? It is okay to say no, because all too often, I cannot. But we need to remind ourselves of this amazing truth each and every day. We belong to God. Therefore, we are already holy. Like it or not.

Holiness does require work on our part. A little cleaning house is always a good thing, because if we want to remain in God, we ought to always be striving to be our best when in his presence — which is always, because God is always with us. Now understand this, please. God does not expect us to approach him all buttoned up, wrinkle-free, and perfect. That is not what I am talking about at all. He calls us just as we are, sinful and broken and wounded. He wants us to bring him all of our mess, but he also wants us to desire that the mess be cleaned up with his help. That the brokenness be fixed. That the wounds be healed. That the sin be wiped away. Being aware of what needs tweaking and changing and fixing and mending and let go of is a beautiful gift, a gentle nudge in the right direction from our Advocate, the Holy Spirit. We are engaged in a fierce battle against the world and the lie that sin is not real and cannot hurt us, which is one of the greatest lies of all. Sin builds up a wall between us and Jesus, and most good relationships tend to last a whole lot longer when you don't have a wall keeping you apart. Kind of an obstacle in the whole intimacy department, wouldn't you agree?

This holiness? It is not about losing yourself, but gaining who you truly are, as you seek out a deeper relationship with Christ. Isn't this why we are so attracted to our own family tree and discovering truths about our ancestors? Real connection to real people and family is as important as chips and salsa. We desire to know where we come from and to whom we belong. As I journey closer to the heart of Christ, and work on my Father-daughter relationship, those areas of "holiness improvement" reveal themselves to me, sometimes more than I like. It is like any relationship, really. When you spend enough time with a person, you learn what they like, what they expect, and how to please them. You also learn quickly what they do not like, such as your oatmeal, or the way you load the dishwasher, or your hideous toothpaste dispensing technique. It isn't a sign of weakness to want to please a lover, to go out of your way for him ... it is a sign of love. Love is not lust or doing what feels good or makes you happy, no matter what the Freeform channel tells you. I prefer to use the Saint Thomas Aquinas definition: love is desiring the greater good for another.

I strive for holiness not to impress others, and not even to impress God (although sometimes I do try to impress him, which as we already discussed is a huge waste of time, but what can I say, I am a slow learner), but rather because I am his beloved and he is mine. Because I belong to him. Because he has set me apart. The greater good? That is eternity in heaven with God. I want that more than that second pitcher of sangria. I want eternity in heaven with God for me, for my husband, and for my children. And for that really cute guy who sold us our Christmas tree at the Home Depot on Sunset Boulevard ten years ago, because, well ... if he had sold you your tree, you would understand why.

The idea of having to give things up that we like and enjoy is not such a popular concept today. The world's mantra is "do whatever makes you happy." The only problem with that is there is a whole buffet of "fun things" out there that might make you happy for a little while, but that in the end only lead you into a pit of misery. Trust me. I have been in that pit. It's not fun. It is kind of like eating an entire pizza when no one is looking. Or spending your entire paycheck on a new wardrobe. Or eating an entire tub of ice cream. Or flirting with men just to prove you are still attractive when you are married. Or eating an entire bag of chips and salsa. Or having that second pitcher of sangria. They all start out fun, but eventually make you sick.

My path to holiness at first felt like a painful stripping of everything I held tight in an attempt to feel good. But I've found it was truly a most needed lesson in the truest things my heart was longing for. Things like self-control, purity, modesty, humility, perseverance, endurance, strength, compassion, and love. I am not saying this path is easy. There are some habits we all have that we absolutely love. Habits that we believe make us who we are. Habits that we know are contrary to what God wants for us, but are just too frightening to let go of. I hate to say it, but these habits, most likely, are our greatest sins, the idols we worship in place of God. Beware, because the enemy who never tires of trying to lure us away from God (a God who is boring and old-fashioned and clearly doesn't want us to enjoy life at all) is exceptionally good at making these sins look harmless, acceptable, and okay. But that is a lie. Sin does harm us. Sin harms everyone. Anything we do that keeps us from a full relationship with our heavenly Father is harmful. Which means those not-so-good things you do or say or look at, or those not-so-good places you go — they are not what make you who you are. You are not your sin. In fact, it is only when you let go of these self-imposed chains that you will finally start living fully the life God created you for. Hard to do? Sugar fudge, yes! But worth it? Oh, sweet friend, I would not be writing today if it were not worth it.

Living in holiness does not mean living in bondage. Living in holiness means at last living in freedom. I promise you, there is nothing creepy about that life of freedom. I am living that life now. While I have been called rowdy, I have never been called creepy.

Did I mention I was once called rowdy? I can't remember. But I have been called other things, as well. Like funny. That's okay by me, because I am sure that Jesus was a funny guy. I am not sure why people think Jesus wasn't funny or that he didn't like to have a good time. Maybe it has to do with how sorrowful his last years of life on earth were. The temptation, the betrayal, the Passion, the crucifixion … certainly, there is no humor in any of that. Maybe people think that because Jesus suffered so much, there was no joy, and if we are to follow him, then we too, must be joyless, must live in a constant state of suffering. I can't even begin to count how many times I have made a joke, only to hear in response, "That's sacrilege." Or how often humor in my writing is misunderstood and taken quite literally and way too seriously. I am sorry, but I personally think there is nothing more tragic than a humorless Catholic! Humor is so good for the soul. I just took two of my kids to see a movie that had us laughing for two hours straight, and when we left my son said, "It feels so good to laugh, doesn't it, Mom?" Yes! Yes it does. Because laughter lifts our spirits and breaks down barriers, and Lord knows I do enough crying, so yes, please, bring on the laughter! Humor is necessary. It opens us up to be better listeners as well as messengers. It has an incredible way of disarming, breaking the ice, and uniting. I have to believe that when we laugh,

God laughs with us. After all, who do you think gifted us with this sense of humor in the first place? Call me crazy, but aren't our God-given gifts meant to be used?

How do I know God was funny? Well, there's the ridiculousness of my own life as proof. I mean, honestly, if I didn't laugh, I would have died from choking on my tears before I turned twenty. But also, if you read the Bible, you can see and hear the humor. A camel fitting through the eye of a needle? Maybe not funny now, but back in the day, that was one funny thing for Jesus to say. How about Sarah and Abraham, way too old to have a baby, and they become pregnant. A super old pregnant lady? That is funny! That is something you might dress up as on Halloween just to get a good laugh. When Sarah gives birth to a boy, they name him Isaac. Do you know what Isaac means in Hebrew? Isaac means, "he laughs." See? God does have a sense of humor. As Sarah says herself, in Genesis 21:6, "God has made laughter for me; everyone who hears will laugh over me."

The Bible is chock-full of joy and laughter, and while Jesus is not like a comedian at open mic night, throwing out joke after joke, he is subtle and witty. Not to mention his use of one-liners is pretty spot on, often directed at the Pharisees, who I am certain were pretty humorless. He is also the guy who turns water into wine when you run out, and not just any cheap wine like I drink, but the good wine, like those fancy people drink. I don't know about you, but I'd totally invite that guy to all of my parties. If picturing an almighty God as being a fun God is hard to do, remember this. He sent us his only Son to be born a baby, a human, innocent and totally dependent on his human mother and foster father. He was born like you and me. He did this so we could trust that he understands us. He experienced everything we experience. He was not only about the sorrow and pain. Jesus had friends, and he went to dinner parties, and he was invited to weddings, and he was a son, and let's be honest, the ladies loved him. If Jesus is like us, then he had every emotion. Even the joyful ones. I imagine that his laugh was beautiful.

I won't lie, because lying is bad, but all too often, I do feel put on the spot for joyfully living out my faith. It goes beyond my battling this fear of people thinking I am a creepy church lady. I can handle people thinking I am creepy, but it is difficult to handle feeling mocked, interrogated, or even put up on a pedestal. Recently on a trip, in a group of adults drinking wine, I mentioned I would be making it to Mass on Sunday if anyone cared to join me. By the end of the night, this one statement earned me the new nickname "the Mother Teresa of the group." Now, if I really wanted to push this holier-than-thou image I felt they had in their minds, I would have corrected them and told them it's "SAINT Teresa of Calcutta." I also contemplated bringing up the fact that Saint Teresa cared for the poorest of the poor, and I was sitting in a hotel bar drinking wine on someone else's tab. But I called on the Holy Spirit, and he instructed me to keep my holy mouth shut. I did, however, finish my wine, and decided to go back up to my room, because honestly? I felt like crying. I know. I always cry. These friends? I do not believe they meant any intentional hurt or harm at all. They are good people who were having fun and who simply have not encountered Christ in a personal way. Yet even knowing this, I still wanted to cry.

Living out your Catholic faith in today's secular world is one fierce battle that, I gotta say, I often feel too weak to fight. Life is so much easier when I stay in my holy huddle or choose to keep quiet. Being bold about my Catholic faith is simple when I remain in my Catholic circle of friends who think as I do. I am tired of having to stick up for my humor, explaining why being funny is not sinful and why God loves me the way I am, and that I am not rowdy but spirit-filled. I grow weary when I find myself in a crowd of people who worship this world and look at me like I am some anti-feminist, crazy Jesus freak who is as outdated as the iPhone 4. If I had a dollar for every time I was told, "You're so good," I'd be a freaking millionaire. The battle to not keep Christ hidden is real. But if I back down and keep quiet, guess who is victorious? I'll give you a hint. It's not me. I refuse to lose. But if I speak up and share my faith and continue to be funny and joyful (which, by the way, is not the same as being rowdy), then Jesus and I have a much better chance of winning the battle.

It is true that I have changed. When I was rescued by Jesus and intentionally chose to pick up my cross daily and follow him, some things had to go. This can be a very painful process, because our habits become such an enormous part of our daily lives. Letting go of something we have trained ourselves to need can feel like removing a limb with our own teeth. But don't let that frighten you. Because ya know what happened? When I let go of lesser things, greater things bloomed in their place. When I removed those walls that stood between my Creator and me, a life of freedom began. Prayers were being answered! Prayers for a stronger marriage, authentic relationships, deeper wells of compassion and understanding, and greater love. Colors became brighter, and a desire to live — to really live — filled my entire heart and soul. I began to thirst for knowledge as I discovered my purpose and worth and my true identity. Bad habits that were fun in the moment but led to deep regret were replaced with a burning and unquenchable desire to continue on this journey closer to the heart of Christ.

The key to continuing on this journey to holiness, to running this race without growing weary, is to put on that battle gear each and every day. All of it. It is also important when I find myself in this battle to remember Ephesians 6:12: "For we are not contending against flesh and blood, but against the principalities, against the powers, against the world rulers of this present darkness, against the spiritual hosts of wickedness in the heavenly places." Those people who mock, judge, label, or put down my new-found zeal for Christ? The world that tells me that if I choose the holy path I will be outdated and an outcast, and that I am better off just going with the flow? The fear that creeps in convincing me that a person like me could never be considered holy? That woman who called me rowdy? These people, this world, that fear, that unacceptable comment from an obviously very unkind woman that I cannot let go of … none of this is what we battle against. Our battle is with the enemy and his army, the evil spirits that surround us and never let up. This is why we must dress for battle, especially as we deepen our relationship with God, because this is precisely what the enemy's schemes are all about: to keep us away from our Father. Why? Because when we choose to be holy and abide in Christ, standing firm with our feet secure in our sandals of peace, what was scattered is gathered, what was lost is found, what was sick is healed, and what was broken is mended.

Our striving for holiness allows those in the dark a glimpse of the light of the Lord. So do not worry what others think, my friend. The only opinion of you that matters is God's, and I happen to know for a fact that his love is wild for you. Even if you are creepy. Especially if you are rowdy.

BATTLE PLAN

I will read the Gospel stories and look for the subtle humor and joy. I will only work on changing those parts of me that are not pleasing to the Lord, and I will stop drinking cheap wine and only drink the good wine ... because that is the wine Jesus brings.

WEAPON OF CHOICE

Strap on those sandals of peace, which ground us in the Good News of the Gospel, fully preparing me to stand my ground when being a bold Catholic feels too difficult. Meditate on Hebrews 12:14. "Strive for peace with all men, and for the holiness without which no one will see the Lord."